REDNECKIN'

REDNECKIN'

*A Hell-Raisin', Foot-Stompin'
Guide to Dancin', Dippin'
and Doin' Around in a
Gen-U-Wine Country Way*

KATHRYN JENSON

*Illustrated by Jim Calhoon
Photographed by Earl Shadden*

A PERIGEE BOOK

Perigee Books
are published by
The Putnam Publishing Group
200 Madison Avenue
New York, New York 10016

Library of Congress Cataloging in Publication Data

Jenson, Kathryn.
  Redneckin' : a hell-raisin', foot-stompin'
guide to dancin', dippin', and doin' around in
a gen-u-wine country way.

  1. Oklahoma—Social life and customs—Anecdotes,
facetiae, satire, etc.   2. Country life—Oklahoma—
Anecdotes, facetiae, satire, etc.   3. Southern
States—Social life and customs—Anecdotes, facetiae,
satire, etc.   4. Country life—Southern States—
Anecdotes, facetiae, satire, etc.   I. Title.
F701.J46   1983   306'.09766   82-18061
ISBN 0-399-50733-7

BOOK DESIGN BY BERNARD SCHLEIFER

First Perigee Printing, 1983

Printed in the United States of America

1 2 3 4 5 6 7 8 9

For *Mama* and *Daddy Grimm*,
Uncommon Common Folk

Acknowledgments

EXTRY SPECIAL THANK-YOU-KINDLYS to my editor, Judy Linden; John Wright, my agent, and Ernestine Miller, who together came up with the idea to do a book on Rednecks and inspired me to use my experience for this one; Nancy Comley; Priscilla Leder; Ron Querry; and David Mair. Also to Linda Grimm, Juanita Lucas, Ed McMillan, Jimmy Joe Peckio, Buddy Baker, Dewell Ray Jenson, Roslyn and Bill Arends at Cowboy Country Western Store in McAlester, OK, Peggy Hall, Chris Fox, Ben Tucker, Keith Shadden, Jack Janszen, Joe Hackworth, Ted Barlow and all the rest at Fluid Haulers, Inc., Isabel Querry, Marty and Maryann Schichtman, Michael Feehan, Michael Donaghe, Joan Worley, Ray Merlock, Laurie Finke, Bob Markley, John W. Grimm II, Tommy Maisano, and all the rednecks who have a-purpose or not a-purpose learned me how.

List of What's Inside

Openin' Words   11

What's a Redneck?   11

What's a Yahoo?   13

1 There Ain't No Reason on God's Earth to be Called by a Name Like Winthrop: Namin' Redneck Style   15

Plain Ol' Names   16
     HORSE COLTS; FILLIES

Two Names Is Sometimes Better'n One   17
     HORSE COLTS; FILLIES

Solvin' a Special Namin' Problem   17

Last Words on Namin'   18

2 Sayin' the Right Thing and Sayin' It Right: Talkin' Redneck Style   19

Sayin' the Right Thing: Phrases Handy as a Pocket on a Shirt   19

Sayin' It Right: "The *Tars* on *Far* Burn Mainly in the *Flars*"   33

Ten Talkin' Right Rules: For the First Thing, There Ain't No "g" in "Fixin'"   37

On Second Thought, Add on These Here Ones   38

**3 You Can Judge a Redneck by His Cover(alls):
Dressin' Redneck Style**   40

The Well-Heeled Redneck: Boot Basics   41

The Well-Dressed Redneck: Body Coverin's   46

It's a Cinch: Belts and Buckles   49

The Crownin' Glory: Hats   50

Little Extries: The Finishin' Touches   52

Monogrammin'   53

They Is One of Us: Redneck Designer Lines   54

**4 Fry a Little Tenderloin:
Eatin' and Cookin' Redneck Style**   55

Eatin' In   55

     CALLIN' YOUR MEALS RIGHT; 10 IMPORTANT
     RULES TO FOLLOW IN COOKIN' AND EATIN';
     COMMON MENU FOR A COMMON DAY; RECEIPTS
     AND COOKIN' INSTRUCTIONS; ADDITIONAL RECEIPTS

Snacks and the Dinner Bucket   73

Eatin' Out   75

     DRIVE-INS; CAFES; BUFFETS

**5 Mobile Home, Sweet Mobile Home:
Housin' Redneck Style**   83

Inside   84

Outside   87

Makin' Your Trailer House More Solid   89

6 I Love My Truck: Travelin' Redneck Style   91

Fancy Rigs   91

Care and Washin' Instructions   92

Some Fittin' Bumper Stickers   93

7 **Payin' the Rent and Havin' Some Fun:**
   Workin' and Playin' Redneck Style   94

Payin' the Rent: Workin' Out Is a Poor Way to
Serve the Lord   94

Tradin': "What You Reckon an ol' Thing Like That's
Worth, Anyways?"   95

Jockeyin' Horses   98

  HORSE CENTS; SELLIN' POINT LINES TO USE

Takin' Up the Slack   100

Havin' Some Fun: What to Do When You Ain't Doin'
Nothin' Is Drinkin' and Dancin'   101

  WHERE-TO: JOINTS, HONKY TONKS, CLUBS AND
  BARS; WHAT-TO: LONGNECK BUD, JACK BLACK,
  BLUE SOCK, CAT WHISKEY AND HOMEMADE
  BEER; EXTRY SPECIAL SECTION: OKLAHOMA
  LIQUOR LAWS; HOW-TO: JUST FOLLOW IN MY
  BOOTSTEPS; TO-WHAT: ANOTHER SOMEBODY DONE
  SOMEBODY WRONG SONG; EXTRY EXTRY SPECIAL
  SECTION: A NIGHT AT THE DEW DROP INN

A Man's a Man For All That   117

  HUNTIN': THAT AIN'T BAMBI, THAT'S DINNER ON
  THE HOOF; TRAPPIN': WHY WOULD A MAN SHOOT
  A TRAP? THEY AIN'T GOOD EATIN' AND THEY'RE
  DEAD ANYWAYS; FISHIN': TROTLINES AND
  TELEPHONIN'

Playin' Smart: Books You Got to Read In   125

The Picture Shows: Movies Rated "R" for Redneck   127

Television: "Dallas" Is Too Rich for Rednecks   128

Places to Visit   129

Big Events You Got to Make   131

  EXTRY SPECIAL EVENT: COW CHIP THROW;
  THE ANYTIME, ANYPLACE EVENT: "LET'S
  RODEO"

8 Usin' Your Head for Somethin' Other'n a Hat Rack: Thinkin' Redneck Style   136

Religion   137

Guns   137

Big Bidness   137

Big Gov'mint   137

Them: Yankees and Other Foreigners   137

Education   138

Kin   138

Life in General   139

9 Little Things Mean a Lot: Points of Style Redneck Style   140

All Them Little Finishin' Touches that Kinely Pulls Things Together   140

DIPPIN' AND CHEWIN' AND ROLLIN' YOUR OWN; WALKIN' AROUND AND JUST STANDIN' STILL; MAKIN' DO; A SPECIAL COMMENT ON BALIN' WIRE; CURES

Stayin' Common   157

Humor in Redneck Form   158

Redneck Mascot: The Armadillo   162

10 Looky Here: Pichur Models You Can Pattern Yourself After   164

Gals   164

THE QUEEN OF THE DEW DROP INN; THE HONKY TONK ANGEL; MAMA; THE WIFE; THE SWEET YOUNG THING; THE GOOD OL' GIRL

Men   170

THE COWBOY; THE ROUGHNECK; THE DRUG STORE COWBOY; THE GOOD OL' BOY; THE URBAN COWBOY; THE WORKIN' MAN

Openin' Words

WHAT'S A REDNECK?

YOU ARE FIXIN' to commence readin' a book that sits out to learn you all there is to know about bein' a redneck. If you already know what bein' a redneck is all about, readin' this prob'ly won't help you none, but it sure as heck won't hurt you none, neither. It never hurts to study up on somethin' even if you're darn good at it already. If, considerin' the other side of the question, you wasn't fortunate enough to be borned and raised up redneck, careful readin' of this here book is a-goin' to uncover a heap of valuable information you can put to real good use if you've a mind to. We're as sure of that fact as we are about the outcome of a wrasslin' match between a big bear and a little bear, when the big bear's got the little bear down.

Now, we ain't claimin' the task before you of a-makin' yourself over into a redneck is goin' to be an easy one. We reckon it's a lot more a chore tryin' to turn a silk purse into a sow's ear than it is to make an effort in the opposite direction. On the other hand, we figger that if you put your mind to it you'll prob'ly be more'n capable, with our help of course, of makin' a respectable start in the right direction. If you was smart enough to buy this here book in the first place, you darn sure ought to be smart enough to do like it says to do. And if you do like it says to do, you'll be redneckin' for sure. We can

almost guaran-darn-tee you that if you don't become a redneck in the altogether, you're more'n likely to at least be
taken for one.

We're a-workin' here from the stand that when you're
talkin' redneck, you're talkin' country and you're talkin' western. Most of all you're talkin' basic. What with all the confusion, hustle and bustle, and just plumb craziness in this
world of ours today, there don't seem nothin' for it but to get
back to basics. And we are here to tole you, there ain't nothin'
more basic than the redneck and the way he lives out the time
he's been given.

Now we ain't no fools, and we know some folks hold that
redneck ain't a particular nice name for a body. Well, we don't
agree. When you're a redneck, things is a lot more simple and
satisfyin'. Your basic redneck is just common folk livin' common style and tryin' the best he can to get along the best he
can. Redneckin' is enjoyin' the simple things in life, workin'
hard, not a-lettin' yourself be bothered by a heap a hard ques-
tions and worrisome ideas, and raisin' a little hell ever now
and then. It's eatin' good ol' American food, dressin' in a way
that looks and feels good, dancin', drivin' a truck, and the like.

Since lottsa folks in this country ain't, as we done already
said, got the advantage of bein' born into a practicin' redneck
family and bein' raised to redneck, those of us more blessed
took to thinkin' we might help 'em out. We ain't interested
one mite in tellin' anybody the way they ought to live; this is a
free country, and we never been ones to poke our noses into
other folks' doin's. We look at what we're aimin' to do here as
kinely puttin' the food on the table so's them that wants to
belly up to it, can. How you take to or put to use the good
advice we're a-fixin' to give you comes under the headin' of
your own business.

We've rounded up information in all the important areas
we could come up with. Each of the sections of this here book
talks about one part of bein' a redneck. We've tried our
darndest to dress the whole hog, but that ain't sayin' you got
to eat it. Grab a pork chop here or a slice a bacon there as the
cravin' strikes and gum around on it a spell. We figger that
once you get a taste of good ol' redneck flavor, you'll make a

pig of yourself a-comin' back for seconds. Now don't get discouraged and holler calf-rope, that is give up, if it all don't go down easy. Even if you can't swallow all we're a-givin' you, what you do get down and keep down is sure to be nourishin'.

As a kind of way into tellin' you what you can do to make yourself over into a redneck, we're a-goin' to begin by settin' out what it is makes folks *not* redneck. These yahoos (pronounced with an *a* like in "may" or "day"), by the light of our way of seein' things, is a large part of what's wrong with this country today. As you read down the list, you might very likely see yourself in it somewheres. Well, if the boot fits, wear it. Half the battle in solvin' a problem is seein' there is one in the first place. You just keep on rememberin' that there ain't nothin' *totally* hopeless and that anybody's got a mind to, can better himself.

WHAT'S A YAHOO?

- Anybody who says "youse guys" rather than "y'all."
- Everybody on welfare ('cept for kin and old folks who ain't got no choice).
- Anybody who'd live in or even go to see the sights of New York City.
- Any man that'd name his boy after himself and put a "II" after the name rather'n "Junior."
- Any woman who don't know how to make buttermilk biscuits and cream gravy and/or don't know how to chicken-fry steak.
- Anybody who don't know the difference 'tween dippin' and chewin'.
- Anybody who'd order a can or a bottle of beer rather'n a long-neck Bud.
- Anybody who don't know how to do the two-step. Not knowin' how to do the Cotton-eye Joe ain't as bad, but it ain't nothin' to be too proud of neither.
- Any man who don't think his mama's the most perfect woman ever walked or drawed breath.
- Any man who ain't never hunted or trapped for his own food.

1

There Ain't No Reason on God's Earth to be Called by a Name Like Winthrop: Namin' Redneck Style

THERE AIN'T NO DENYIN' that you'd a stood a better chance of growin' up redneck and not havin' to bother studyin' so hard on this here book if you'd a been named redneck style to commence with. Now, we ain't a-tryin' to fault your mama and daddy none for what they prob'ly did with only the best intentions. Chances are they didn't know no better'n to give you the name you got if you ain't got one like the ones we give out here.

We've rounded up some fine examples of names that anybody with a lick a sense would be more'n proud to bear, figgerin' that the best place to start this chore of you becomin' a redneck is with the changin' of your name. Even supposin' you don't have a mind to go to all the trouble of changin' your

name down at the court house, you can just kinely start thinkin' of yourself by one of these here possibilities and askin' them that's close to you to do likewise. It don't hardly seem likely to hurt none, and it's bound to help you get started.

We figger givin' out these names will allow you to plan for the future of your young 'uns, too. You can make things a darn sight easier for them by namin' 'em right as they come out of the gates, even if the same wasn't done for you. We all know that most folks want their young 'uns to have it easier and better'n they did. Well, givin' your own little cookie-crumblin' rug-rat one of these here names will help you do just that.

We've divided up the names into three groups to make your choicin' easier. The first group's made up of plain ol' names, and it's kinely sub-divided into one list for the little fillies and one for the little horse colts. The second group shows you that even a name that don't exactly melt your butter upon first hearin' can really shine out with the addin' of a second part. The third group offers up some namin' suggestions to help you deal with a special problem.

PLAIN OL' NAMES

Horse Colts

Alva	Cloyd	Doyce	Eulus	Murl	Romayne
Arvil	Coy	Dub	Gailard	Nolen	Royce
Azel	Delbert	Durcie	Gaylen	Novis	Thetchel
Bozell	Dester	Eldean	Homer	Odell	Tink
Buel	Deward	Elgert	Jethro	Ollie	Veri
Buford	Dewayne	Emery	Jewell	Olvin	Vestal
Burl	Dewell	Emmitt	Kermit	Oran	Vestel
Cledith	Dewey	Eudell	Larvel	Orval	Virgil
Cletis	Dewitt	Euel	Leland	Otho	Willard
Clovus	Doss	Eulan	Luster	Quenith	

Fillies

Allcie	Cleola	Dayna	Eula	Idella	Izoral
Beulah	Cleota	Derothia	Floy	Ima	Jaquita
Blanquitta	Cloweta	Dixiola	Graceva	Inabell	Jawanda
Burma	Darthulia	Elotila	Gwenda	Irlene	LaDawn

LaHoma	Leoma	Myrtilla	Rhenia	Tycene	Wretha
LaVerna	Letha	Noriva	Rosella	Ura	Wynema
LaVesta	Loretta	Oleta	Starla	Velma	Zelma
LaVonne	Lorine	Ozelle	Tempest	Veranda	
LaWanda	Lurline	Rebellea	Texal	Verna	
Legartha	Mada	Redeen	Twana	Wanelle	

TWO NAMES IS SOMETIMES BETTER'N ONE

Horse Colts

Billy Bob	Jimmy Lee
Billy Frank	John Willy
Billy Jack	Johnny Bill
Bobby Joe	Lee Roy
Jim Bob	Sammy Ray

Fillies

Bobbie Dawn	Katy Lou
Bobbie Jean	Lillie Opal
Cora Mae	Ora Lue
Dovie Jewell	Vorlia May
Ida Mae	Wordie Bea

SOLVIN' A SPECIAL NAMIN' PROBLEM

This here extry special list shows you what you can do if you're a daddy and you don't get blessed with no horse colt to name after yourself. This is somethin' nobody likes much to think on, of course, but there is just no foreseein' the mysterious ways of Mama Nature; a man's got to be ready for the worst.

Daddy's Name	Filly's Version	Daddy's Name	Filly's Version
Alfonso	Alfonza	Joe	Joetta
Art	Artalee	Marvin	Marvayne
Ben	Benella	Ralph	Ralphetta
	Benetta	Ray	Raelyn
	Beneva		Rayette
Berl	Berlynne	Rick	Ricketta
Charles	Charla	Rock	Rockolynne
Don	Donalee	Ron	Roneva
Earl	Earlene	Verl	Verlena
Ed	Edlean	Vern	Vernita
	Edlena	Wayne	Waynelle
Gayle	Gaylavonne		

Now, of course, this a-namin' your young 'uns after yourself can get plumb out of hand. We personally knowed of a man named Hubert had five kids. He named the first four, which was all girls:

Huberta
Huberteva
Hubertilla
Hubertetta

By the time he got his fifth and last child, his only boy, Hubert clearly lost sight of reality. Rather'n just bein' satisfied to stick plain ol' Hubert on the boy and be done with it, Hubert called him Huberton! This is really pretty close to a-goin' too far. Folks could go to talkin'.

LAST WORDS ON NAMIN'

- If you get one boy and one gal, go on and name 'em after you and the wife both. For instance, if you're "Azel," your boy's "Li'l Azel," and if the wife's "Darthulia," your gal's "Li'l Darthulia." Put that "Li'l" in front to keep straight who you're a-talkin' about or a-callin' to dinner or chores.
- Don't never, under no circumstances, number your boy. Puts folks in mind of the numberin' tags they hook onto a steer's ear when they're a-runnin' him through the sale barn.

2

Sayin' the Right Thing and Sayin' It Right: Talkin' Redneck Style

SAYIN' THE RIGHT THING: PHRASES HANDY AS A POCKET ON A SHIRT

ANYBODY WHO EVER TRIED to learn a foreign tongue knows that if a person works at it hard enough and long enough, he's bound to get some of it stuck into his head. Now, we got a language all our own, and after a-listenin' to them who don't speak redneck a-flappin' their jaws, we figger it's goin' to seem like a foreign language to them. And in this particular case, them might very well be you.

We're now a-goin' to load you up with a peck sack full of phrases that rednecks use anytime most anything needs discussin' or commentin' on. We always reckoned it was a pure-D waste of time a-worryin' and a-frettin' tryin' to come up with a good way to say somethin' when there's so many tried and true ways already there for the usin'.

Since most of y'all ain't a-goin' to be real familiar with these phrases you're fixin' to get loaded up with, we're a-settin' up the situation they could be used in and doin' some explainin' when necessary. We think we've given you enough to cover just about everything from sittin' around after supper chewin' the fat, to goin' out for a big time evenin' of two-steppin' at your local Dew Drop Inn.

We'll commence with an easy one. Just suppose you was sittin' around the ol' spit-and-whittle bench on Main Street with a bunch of the boys and doin' a little bench rodeoin'. Now suppose that y'all couldn't help but notice a-passin' by this young heifer not blessed with an overload of good looks. You might not know it, but you got at your disposal a large variety of ways to comment on this to them that cares to listen. We'll just list 'em out now, so's you can get the general idea:

> "Whew! She's so ugly she'd make a freight train take a dirt road."
>
> "She's been beat severely with the ugly stick."
>
> "Boy, oh, boy! How'd you like to have a litter out of that?"
>
> "Now I reckon that pore thing cain't help how she looks, but she sure could stay to home, and that's a fact."
>
> "She's so ugly she'd have to sneak up on the dipper to get a drink from the well." (If you ain't fortunate enough to have a well, you might want to modern this up a bit and make it, "She's so ugly she'd have to sneak up on the sink to get a glass of water." It all amounts to about the same thing.)

We kinely set this next one aside on account of it's bein' pretty darn powerful. We don't suggest tossin' it around except in extreme cases. Someone who qualifies for this one is prob'ly a-goin' to fall into one of two categories. She might be what we call a "two-sacker," which is a gal so ugly you got to wear a paper sack on your head whilst you're makin' love just in case hers happens to fall off. Worst than that, she may be flat out "coyote ugly." A gal that bad lookin' is one that when you wake up next to her in the daylight and she's a-layin' on your arm, you'll chew your arm off to keep from wakin' her up a-movin' it.

> "She's so ugly her daddy had to tie pork chops around her neck when she was a baby so's the dogs would play with her."

Movin' on to more pleasurable things, let's suppose on the other hand that you and the boys see strollin' by a sweet young thing lookin' real good, a for-certain contender for Miss Rodeo America. In that case, you got your choice of the followin':

"I been to two county fairs, a goat ropin', and a punkin rollin' and I ain't *never* seen nothin' like *that* before."

"She's as shiny as a new dime in a goat's butt."

"She's cuter'n a bug's ear."

"There ain't nothin' wrong with that, now, is there?"

"She's as cute as a speckled pup under a red wagon."

"She's built like a brick shit house."

If you happen to get a whiff of whatever foo-foo juice she's a-squirted on herself, and it smells read good, try:

"She smells like a lady a-goin' to meetin'."

If she's dressed to kill:

"She's sure enough dressed up like a mule in buggy harness."

If the little lady ain't exactly little:

"She's so fat that when her daddy tells her to haul ass, she's got to make two trips."

"The rear end of her pants looks like a tow sack with two hogs a-wrasslin' in it."

Changin' the scene some, let's suppose you was a-needin' to let the folks you was a-talkin' to know that the person you was a-talkin' about wasn't too long on smarts:

"He's about half a bubble off."

"He don't know if he's a-washin' or a-hangin' out."

"If you put his brains in a bluebird, it'd fly backwards."

"He's a few bricks shy of havin' a full load."

"I reckon his mama dropped him head first on the wood pile directly after he was born."

"He's got rooms to let upstairs."

"Not only does he not know much, he don't even suspect a hell of a lot."

"He lacks a few straws of havin' a full bale."

"He's kinely like a hog; the good Lord put his head on the wrong end too."

"He's so stupid he couldn't roll rocks down a steep hill."

"He's a little short 'tween the ears."

"He ain't got the sense God gave a goose."

"He's kinely like a goose; he wakes up in a new world every day."

If the person under discussion ain't so much dumb as plumb loco:

"He's as crazy as a March hare."

"He don't know the meanin' of normal."

You'll prob'ly notice right off that this here next category is kinely sparse. It's the one you look to when you're a-needin' to mention that someone's real smart. Comparin' the number of possibilities here with the number in the two categories above ought to tell you somethin', oughtn't it?

"She was so bright her mama had to put a #3 washtub over her head each mornin' so's the sun would come out."

Now, if you happen to run across a person who is real skittish or nervous:

> "He was nervous as a painted woman in church."

> "She was so nervous she could thread a sewin' machine and it a-runnin'."

> "He was as nervous as a long-tailed cat in a room full of rockin' chairs."

If yourself or another is feelin' or lookin' particularly happy:

> "I'm as contented as a dead hog in the sun."

> "He was grinnin' like a possum eatin' shit."

> "That really melts my butter."

When you're way past ready to chow down:

> "I'm so hungry I could eat a horse and it a-runnin'."

> "I'm gettin' kinely narrer in the flanks."

> "That's done flung a cravin' on me."

> "I could eat the south end of a north bound pole cat."

> "I'm so hungry my stomach thinks my throat's been cut."

When you been treated to some fine tastin' vittles:

> "That's right handy to swaller."

> "That tastes so good it makes you want to slap your granny."

When you've ate just about all you can stand:

> "I'm as full as a tick."

> "I'm a-goin' to have to quit on account of my health."

If you're a-eatin' out somewheres and your meat ain't cooked enough:

> "Hon, if you bring me a Band-Aid, I think I can save this here steer."

> "I've had cows hurt worse'n this that recovered."

> "If I got caught eatin' this steak in somebody's pasture, I could be arrested for rustlin'."

> "All they done to this one was knock the horns off."

When folks drop by to visit a spell:

> "Y'all make yourselfs to home."

When they're gettin' ready to leave out:

> "Y'all come, y'hear?"

If they don't seem over willin to head that-a-way, or they is plumb impossible to get rid of:

> "Mama, let's go to bed so's these nice folks can go home."

If you're the one doin' the leavin' out from someone else's place:

> "Y'all might as well come go with me, now."

If you got the need to indicate your own limits:

> "I can sure read writin', but I can't write readin' much."

If you want to let someone know yourself or somebody else is flat busted out:

> "He's so poor he can't even change his mind."

> "I'm too broke to pay attention."

> "He's so poor, the bank won't even let him draw breath."

"I'm drove up so tight a tornado couldn't drive a straw through me."

Or to tell off on somebody that he's far from bein' busted out on account of never havin' been too free with his coins:

"He's as tight as the bark on a tree."

"He's so tight he wouldn't pay a nickel to see a pissant eat a bale of hay."

"He's so tight he don't even breathe all the air he needs."

"He really squeezes that ol' eagle 'till it hollers."

If you're called upon to comment on somebody who ain't packin' a lot of extry flesh on their frame:

"He was so thin that when he turned sideways and stuck out his tongue, he looked like a zipper."

"He was so thin he only had one side."

"He was so thin he had to stand up twice to cast a shadder."

"He was so thin that when he drunk a bottle of strawberry sody pop he looked like a thermometer."

"He looks like a red worm with the shit flung out of him."

For assorted leavin'-out-from-somewheres situations:

"Let's adios this joint."

"He was really gatherin' up some of that yonder."

"He's done kicked over the traces."

"He was rarin' to go, but couldn't go for rarin'."

When you need to tell someone that the sauce you're a-drinkin' is mighty powerful stuff:

"That'll sure wind your watch."

"A few drinks of that and you're nine feet tall and bulletproof."

"That ol' stuff'll jump your IQ fifty points real fast."

"That stuff'll make you act single, see double and pay triple."

When you or somebody else has over-indulged in the sauce:

"I'll drive. I'm too drunk to sing."

"He's higher'n a hen's ass at a dead run."

"He was high as a peckerwood hole."

"She was whizzed up pretty good."

When you're feelin' the painful aftereffects of a night or two of heavy drinkin':

"I feel like I been rode hard and put up wet."

"I feel like I been jerked through a knothole backards."

"I feel rough as a cob."

"I feel like I been sent for and couldn't come."

If you need to let a person know that you're downright aggravated with 'em, or that somebody else is, or that somebody's just plumb upset with things in general:

"He was so mad he was a-seein' brass gnats."

"He was hot as a two-dollar pistol."

"She was hot enough to make love to."

"I'm goin' to kill her and tell God she died."

"I'm goin' to quit you like a dead horse does a wagon."

"I'm off a you like a doctor is a dead man."

"You really ripped your drawers with me this time, pard."

"That makes my rear want to dip snuff."

"I'm as mad as a wet settin' hen."

If somebody ain't big on size:

"She's no bigger'n the hammer on a twenty-two."

"He's no bigger'n a bar a soap that's been used all day."

"She's no bigger'n a minute."

When you're a-tryin' to point out that an ol' boy or gal's been less than pure-D faithful to their spouse:

"She was skatin' around on him."

"He was chippin' around on her."

"She's been out high-bobbin' around."

"She was sure enough slippin' around, now."

To give comfort to the spouse who's done found out about what's been a-goin' on in the same situation:

"You'll never miss a slice from a cut loaf."

If somebody's a-gripin' about somethin' that ain't all that much to gripe about:

"Why, I've had worst on my lip and kept a-whistlin'."

When you're tellin' about somebody who was a-pourin' on the tears or hollerin' over somethin':

"She was a-bawlin' and a-slingin' snot every which way."

"He was squealin' like a stuck pig."

If you run on to some woman who's got a slew of young 'uns:

"She's got enough kids to bait a trotline."

"She's got a whole field crew there."

Dependin' on how things is a-goin', of course, to answer the question of "How are you doin'?":

> "I'm shittin' in tall cotton."

> "I'm a-makin' out like a tall dog."

> "I'm kinely like the ol' share cropper. . . . I never had less and enjoyed it more."

> "I'm as fine as a frog hair split four ways and sanded."

> "Can't complain, and wouldn't do no good anyways."

When you're talkin' on a person who's plumb mean:

> "He'll kill anybody big enough to die."

> "He's tougher'n a tombstone."

> "She's as mean as cat crap."

> "He's about half outlaw, now."

> "It ain't that he's mean, exactly, but the mean ones don't mess with him."

> "He was so mean that when he went into the woods he always took a big stick, 'cause he was worried he'd shit wildcats."

> "He wasn't what you'd call mean, but I sure ain't goin' lookin' for one meaner."

If you're discussin' somebody who's just a mite crooked:

> "He's slippery as a hog on ice."

> "He's so crooked he'd cheat his own self if he thought he could get away with it."

When somebody asks you to help out a-doin' somethin' and you don't rightly feel like it:

> "If you want a good hand, look to the end of your arm."

If you got a need for some attention-gettin' threats:

> "I'm goin' to whup knots on your head faster'n you can rub 'em."

> "I'm fixin' to whup your butt, or God's a possum."

> "I'm fixin' to dot your eyes."

"I'm goin' to slap your head up to a peak then slap the peak off."

"I'm goin' to whup you and make you like it."

"I'm goin' to whup you or get whupped a-tryin'."

If you spot an ol' boy who's showin' the signs of agin':

"He's got so many wrinkles on his forehead, he'd have to screw his hat on."

To indicate you been taken aback or plumb shocked at somethin':

"Well, drag me in the bushes and leave me for ripe."

"Well, shoot me a-runnin'."

"Now if that don't beat all I ever slept with." (Course, some folks who ain't real particular can't toss this last one around too freely and remain honest.)

If you need a real show-stopper compliment for an ol' gal:

"You don't sweat much for a fat woman."

If an ol' gal's a pretty fair hand at cookin':

"She can make cream gravy that won't don't."

When you feel the need to brag a bit on your abilities in the sack, keepin' in mind, of course, the notion that them that can do don't often feel the need to say much about it:

"I'm a-fixin' to put a bow in her back, a smile on her face, and change in her pocket."

"I'm a-fixin' to put a smile on your face and a bounce in your walk."

If somebody comes right back a-tellin' you that braggin' often takes the place of doin', you can hit 'em with:

"It's a poor dog won't wag its own tail."

If somebody's a-dishin' out the baloney sauce:

"Don't be pissin' down my back and tellin' me it's a-rainin'."

If you come near to bein' bad hurt a'-doin' somethin':

> "I durn near broke my rear and all its fixtures."

If you're braggin' on somebody for bein' a good worker:

> "There ain't no lazy about him."

> "He'll work from can to can't."

To tell somebody he's more trouble'n he's worth:

> "You're excess baggage, and I can't afford the freight."

If you're a-talkin' about somebody slow as molasses in December:

> "He's so slow he couldn't scatter shit with a rake."

> "He's so slow you got to drive a stake up next to him to see if he's moved at all."

> "He's only got two speeds: slow and slower."

If you're gettin' tired of listenin' to somebody complain:

> "You'd gripe if they hung you with a new rope."

If you send somebody to do somethin' for you, and he don't return for a long while:

> "Well, I hope if they ever decide to hang me, they send you to buy the rope."

To really let a person know you're a lifelong friend:

> "Long's I got a biscuit, you got half."

If you're feelin' kinely depressed and don't mind folks a-knowin' it:

> "My heart's heavy as a bucket a hog livers."

If you run across somebody who's such a piss-poor shot he couldn't hit the broad side a the barn:

> "He couldn't hit a bull in the ass with a bass fiddle."

When somebody's a-wishin' for somethin' that you know ain't even a possible come-true:

> "Yeah, and if frogs had wings they wouldn't bump their butts when they jumped, either."

When you go into a store or office and need to ease into a conversation with the clerk or secretary:

> "You workin' hard or hardly workin'?"

When somebody's smart-alecky enough to comment on your shirt or britches bein' not real clean, you can come back with:

> "No sense wearin' it out a-washin' it."

If you happen across somethin' a-layin' in the road with no real sign that it's owned by anybody:

> "I think I'll just get that 'fore somebody steals it."

When you're plumb wore out:

> "I'm so tired I'm makin' three tracks."

When you're a-plannin' to sell an ol' truck or somethin':

> "I think I'll just turn that ol' truck green."

If somebody's a-pokin' and a-pryin' into your affairs:

> "That comes under the headin' a *my* bidness."

> "You writin' a book, or what?"

When somebody you're a-talkin' to keeps a-lookin' at his watch:

> "You takin' medicine regular?"

When somebody's a-flappin' his jaws when he oughtn't to be:

> "Don't go runnin' your head, now."

> "That's your rear talkin'; your mouth knows better."

> "Don't let your lioness mouth overload your mockin'bird rear, now."

When you're a-tryin' to make a move on an ol' gal:

> "Would you like to waltz across Texas with me on my 54″ × 76″?" (the size of a standard mattress).

> "You know, if you was a-layin' up against my back, you could easily turn my stomach."

> "I think you and me ought to get somethin' straight between us, sug." ('Nough said?)

Dependin' on the situation, if you need to call up an insult right quick:

> "I wisht he was mine, 'cause if he was I'd trade him for a dog and shoot the dog."

> "He ain't exactly chicken shit, but he's sure got hen house ways."

When you're a-feelin' kinely like philosophizin':

> "Life is like bein' on a mule team. If you ain't the lead mule, all the scenery looks the same."

> "What goes 'round comes 'round."

> "If you don't know no difference, it don't make none."

If an ol' gal out at a joint asks if you're married:

> "No, but my wife is."

We'll end up this here section with some suggestions of redneck words what you can use to refer to various types a folks:

Your friend	"My pard"
	"My runnin' buddy"
Your brother	"My bud"
An acquaintance	"A good ol' boy"
	"An outlaw"
Your wife	"The ol' lady"
	"Mama"
	"My kid's mama"
	"The wife"
A gal not your wife	"A filly"
	"A sweet thing"
	"A little heifer"
	"A dirty-legged duck"
	"A skirt"
	"A little dumplin'"
	"A little lady"
	"A skillet"

SAYIN' IT RIGHT: "THE TARS ON FAR BURN MAINLY IN THE FLARS"

Once you got the phrases down pat, you can get right to work on sayin' the words right that go into the phrases. This here little pronouncin' dictionary ought to help you out plenty

there. It shows you how to say the words and gives out an example of usin' 'em to avoid any confusion. This ain't like a regular dictionary where you got to know how to spell a word 'fore you can look it up. These words is spelled exactly how they sound, so there oughtn't to be any problem a-usin' it. Course, we got so many different things to be a-workin' on in the chore of learnin' you to be redneck that we ain't got the time nor the space to be as thorough as Mr. Webster, but we figger you can get the general idea and apply it yourself to them words we leave out.

Ackrit: That there story ain't exactly ackrit, now.

Agg: I injoy a agg with my bacon.

Agin: If you ain't fer me, you're agin me.

Aints: Them aints is all over my kitchen countertop.

Arnin: Most days most women got to do some arnin even though lots a clothes is permnent prest these days.

Ars: All a them young 'uns is ars.

Ast: He ast me four dollars fer that ol' tar.

At: Don't you be a-doin' me like at.

Baggin: I'm a-baggin' you please not to go and do that.

Battry: That ol' battry's dead as a doornail.

Bidness: Big bidness is takin' over the country.

Bobwar: Ain't that the purtiest bobwar fince you ever did see?

Borry: I'm only astin' to borry the durn tractor fer a month.

Bub: We ain't got a light bub in the house.

Chaince: He ain't got a ice cube's chaince in hell.

Cheer: Sit down in that cheer and take a load off a your mind.

Clumb: When I seed that ol' dog was after me, I clumb up that ol' tree in a New York minnit.

Conner: He took that conner on two tars.

Crick: I plumb soaked my britches gittin' acrost that crick.

Daintz: Would you keer to daintz, ma'am?

Dreckly: I'll see to that dreckly after I'm done eatin'.

Druther: I'd druther not.

Errol: I gotta go put a TV errol on the ruf.

Extry: He'll give you a little extry fer your money.

Fanger: He's got his ol' fanger in ever pie in town.

Far: Put a log on the far.

Fince: Come go with me and hep me stretch this fince war.

Flars: Givin' the wife a bookay a flars is real smart.

Foller: Don't you foller me out a here, y'hear?

Frash: Frash aggs is the best.

Fur: It ain't fur from here to there.

Furriner: This country is plumb overrun with furriners of all makes and models.

Ginerly: I don't ginerly do this, but seein' as it's you, I will.

Git: Git that ol' hound out a the house this minnit.

Grain: She was grain with envy.

Hail: Like hail you will.

Hard: You seen my new hard hand around anywheres?

Hep: It's a pore friend won't hep you whin you need it.

Hern: That's hern not yourn.

Hit: Hit ain't hard to do a'tall.

Holler: His head's holler as a gourd.

Holt: Jest grab holt and don't let go for nothin'.

Hunnert: He paid me out in hunnert dollar bills.

Idy: I got an idy this here'll work if it's applied right.

Innersted: I ain't innersted in nothin' you got to say.

Jest: Jest hold your horses, now.

Keer: And I don't keer if you do, neither.

Kin: Kin you believe what you're a-hearin?

Kitch: I'm a-going to kitch hail whin I git to the house.

Lack: She acks jest lack her mama did whin she was her age.

Laig: Don't you be a-pullin my laig.

Liberry: Them liberry books is overdue.

Mall: He lives one mall down that ol' dirt road.

Mare: The mare of our town don't know the meanin' a honest.

Mere: It's seven years bad luck to break a mere.

Nar: This road is durn sure too nar for two trucks to pass.

Nup: Nup, I ain't a-goin' to do it.

Opsit: Whatever you say, he's sure to say the opsit.

Overhauls: He was a-wearin' his new overhauls last evenin'.

Pank: Pank's a good color fer you.

Peert: I ain't feelin' real peert this mornin'.

Piller: There ain't nothin' like a feather piller for sleepin'.

Plars: Hand me up them plars so's I kin fix this here leak.

Probly: She'll prob'ly not make it out tonight.

Puppit: That preacher was a-givin' 'em hell from his puppit.

Purdy: Ain't that purdy, though?

Raglar: I eat three meals a day, raglar.

Ranch: I'll need a ranch to tighten this up with.

Rang: Stay clear a her. She's a wearin' a weddin' rang.

Rassle: I don't want to fight with you, sugar, but I'd love to rassle a spell.

Rat cheer: I was borned rat cheer in this house.

Rinch: I got to rinch these clothes out.

Salry: Carrots and salry is rabbit food.

Sangle: I'm a sangle man, myself.

Seerl: Seerl ain't enough for a real man's breakfast.

Seppin: The whole family was there seppin' for Orval.

Shadder: He's skeered a his own shadder.

Shar: I'm going to take a shar and change my clothes.

Shurf: We got one mean shurf a-runnin' this town.

Skint: He skint that squirrel in no time flat.

Sody: Without sody, biscuits don't raise up.

Sourdeans: Crackers and sourdeans goes good together.

Sprang: Come the sprang a the year, flars grow.

Sumpin: Sumpin' ain't exackly right here.

Surp: Real maple surp's hard to come by.

Swaller: Take you a swaller a that wiz, if you want.

Tar: That tar's got a slow leak.

Tard: I'm so tard I kin't hardly sleep.

Thanks: She thanks she's smarter'n most folks.

Thar: I'll be thar dreckly.

Thoe: Thoe me that piller over here, would you?

Tomar: I'll do it tomar if I ain't got time today.

Turrble: He took a turrble headache last night.

Vydock: They're a-fixin' the vydock on Main Street.

War: Balin' war's handy for fixin' most thangs.

Whal: Come rest yoursef fer a whal.

Whur: Whur you been a-hidin' yoursef?

Widder: He's cranky as an ol' widder woman.

Winder: Open up that winder so's we kin git some air.

Woeman: Let's you and me talk woeman to woeman.

Worsh: He wadn't much of a one to worsh dishes.

Wunst: I was only wrong wunst, and that was whin I thought I was.

Yeller: His face was yeller as a punkin.

Yistiddy: I might ought a took keer a that yistiddy.

Yit: I ain't ready yit.

Yurp: Yurp's a continent overseas.

Zat: Zat a fack?

TEN TALKIN' RIGHT RULES: FOR THE FIRST THING, THERE AIN'T NO "G" IN "FIXIN'"

1. Don't never say the "g" on the end of words endin' with "ing." For instance:

   "I'm fixin' to mosey on over to mama's."

   "Don't be lettin' your mouth overload your rear."

2. Take your time a-talkin'. Folks'll figger you're a-thinkin' about what you're a-sayin' if you keep your speakin' pace at a slow canter rather'n runnin' at a full trot.

3. No matter if you're a-talkin' about man, woman, child, horse, or pickup, put the word "ol'" in front of your nouns. For instance:

   "Ol' Dorvayne never knew what hit him when that ol' pony rared up and headed for nowheres fast."

4. Try not to commit yourself too close to no more'n you absolutely have to. Rely on "should" rather'n "can" or "will." For instance:

   Q. "Will these ol' tars you're a-sellin' get a few more miles?
   A: "They should."

   Q: "Can you make it to church this Sunday?"
   A: "I should be able to, yes."

5. For a nice and easy rhythm to your talkin', use the "a" sound before all them "ing" words you're a-sayin' without the "g." For instance:

   "He was a-talkin' and a-wavin' his arms like he was a-testifyin' way up there in Amen corner."

6. Try not to look the person you're a-talkin' to too hard in the eyes. They'll darn sure figger you're a-lyin' if you do. Look around you ever now and then. It's al-

ways a good idea to kinely know what's happenin' close around you anyways, so's you don't get snuck up on.

7. Put your ol' accent or emphasis on the first syllable of most words with two or more. For instance:

July . . . . *Ju*ly
Umbrella . . . . *Um*brella
Insurance . . . . *In*surance

8. Wipe the words "there is" plumb out a your word collection. Substitute "they are" or "it ain't" dependin' on your meanin'. For instance:

"This is the best beer they are."

"It ain't nothin' to doin' this."

9. Don't never just say you got "paid in cash." It's got to have a "the" in front of it. For instance:

"The ol' IRS don't know nothin' about the jobs I been paid in the cash for."

10. Don't never say you "got" or "have" an affliction of any sort. Instead, say, for instance:

"I took a headache real bad."

"I took the flu last evenin'."

ON SECOND THOUGHT, ADD ON THESE HERE ONES

11. Don't go pronouncin' the "ed" on the back end of in-the-past words like it was a man's name. That sound, redneck style, is more that of a "t." For instance:

Wasted . . . . Wastit
Ruined . . . . Ruint
Skinned . . . . Skint

It won't hurt nothin' to throw in a "t" at the end of some a them "s" endin' words, neither. For instance:

Across.................................Acrost
Unless.................................Unlest

12. Don't skimp none on syllables. If you can kinely throw in a extry one now and then, them short words'll sound more like the long 'uns worth twice as much. For instance:

Head...................................Hay-id
Umbrella........................Um-burr-el-la
Arthritis........................Ar-thur-ite-us
Athlete...........................Ath-uh-leet

13. To make sure you finally do get through a-talkin' sometime and to kinely balance things out, run together a few words with a bunch of syllables. For instance:

Firearms...............................Farms

3

You Can Judge a Redneck by his Cover(alls): Dressin' Redneck Style

BEARIN' THE RIGHT KIND of name and talkin' so's folks can gather up what you're talkin' about is a real good start to goin' redneck. But your good start out of the gates ain't goin' to mean a darn thing if you don't keep movin' on down the track at a pretty fair clip. Next thing to worry about is riggin' yourself out so's you look like what you're named and talkin' like.

Before you can ever dress right, you got to get it plumb out of your head that shirts got to have little gators or ponies sewed on 'em. Way we figger is that the good Lord made ponies to be rode and traded and gators so's they could give up their hides to some of the prettiest, best-wearin' cowboy boots you ever did see. We don't mind an occasional western shirt showin' off a horse or two, but they look plumb silly sittin' there above a man's heart on one of them golf shirts.

The information in this part of the book covers the whole redneck, from head to toe and everything in betweens. We're goin' to take the logical approach to this here subject, figgerin' that workin' from the ground up makes the most sense. Kinely like buildin' a house by startin' with the foundation, we're goin' to start with the boots.

THE WELL-HEELED REDNECK: BOOT BASICS

Merle Haggard said it right in "Okie from Muskogee," when he claimed that in that town boots was still the only manly footwear. Well, Muskogee, Oklahoma, U.S.A. ain't the only place where folks feel this-a-way. No true redneck'd be caught dead or even drunk in a pair of brogans or sandals. And, far as we're concerned, loafers is what lazy people are. The *kind* of boot a man wears depends, of course, on what he's got in mind to be doin' and on his personal taste and bank account.

WORK BOOTS: PLAIN AND SIMPLE

For a work boot, there ain't nothin' to beat a plain ol' short-top cowhide with a ropin' heel and toe. A man can't tend to business if he's worryin' about gettin' his boots scufft up or plumb ruint.

DRESS BOOTS: EXOTICS

These is a whole other matter altogether, with a endless variety of skins, hides and styles to choose from. The only two considerations in the choicin' are how much a man's willin' to pay and what's available in his size. This last consideration's a big one now-a-days, since everyone back east and out west has finally got smart and took to wearin' boots and hats. This has made it kinely tough on those of us who was country when country wasn't cool, but like the existence of this here book suggests, we're a-willin' to share the wealth.

In addition to fancy cowhide dress boots, you got your choice of several of what are called "exotic" leathers or skins. All of these come from animals not as homey as the ol' cow. The most popular are:

Ostrich: Comes in short and long quill. This here is the best wearin' boot they are. Some folks claim the little bumps left where the quills been plucked out put them in mind of chigger or skeeter bites or of a young 'un with a bad skin problem, but we can't see it.

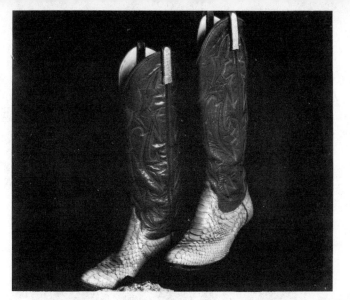

Anaconda: Real pretty but don't wear none too well. The little scales come off if you scrape 'em against much of anything.

Alligator and Crocodile: These are some of your highest priced boots, but they're darn sure worth every penny 'cause they look good and wear even better. Alligator don't wear quite so good as crocodile, 'cause where the gator's got gristle in the joints of his hide, the croc's got bone.

Elephant: Tough with a dull finish and a pretty pattern in the hide.

Eel: Real easy to tear. Eel skin is tissue paper thin, so a man's got to step careful when wearin' these boots. They take a shine best of any of the exotics.

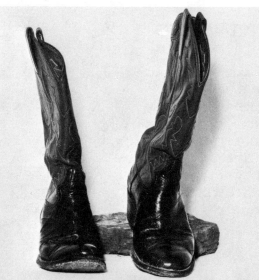

Python: Not as likely to peel off as Anaconda, but you still got to be careful.

Lizard: Several varieties to choose from. In addition to the regular ol' critter, there's ringtail and hornback. Each one's got a different skin pattern.

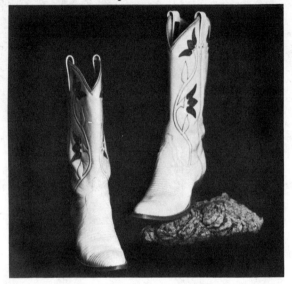

There's also boots made from antelope, anteater, water buffalo, and even chicken and frog skin. These ain't all that common, though, especially the last two mentioned. We figger the ones we talked on before is exotic enough for most rednecks.

THE TOTAL BOOT

1. Mule-ear pulls
2. Bullet-hole pulls
3. Shank
4. Shank stitchin'
5. Toe cap
6. Vamp
7. Bug and Wrinkle stitchin'

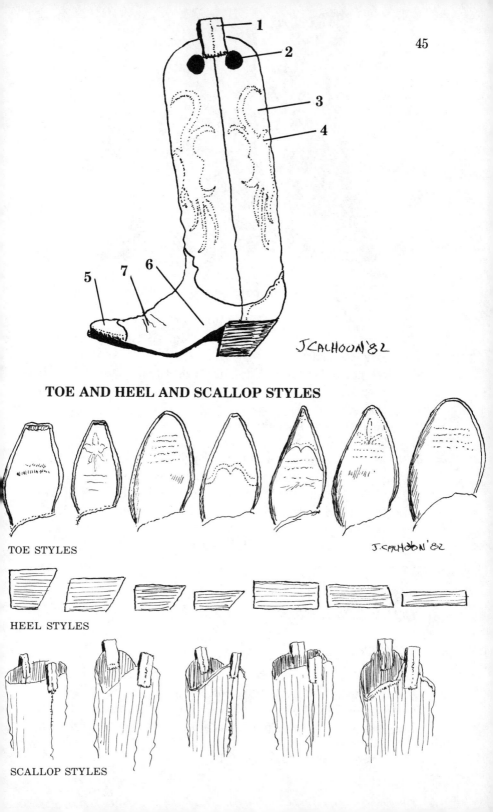

45

TOE AND HEEL AND SCALLOP STYLES

TOE STYLES

HEEL STYLES

SCALLOP STYLES

TAKIN' CARE OF 'EM PROPER

- Use a light cream polish and don't use too much.
- To keep 'em lookin' new, polish the sides of the soles and the heels with hoof black.
- Never polish the tops. First, it'll ruin the stitchin'. Second, it's a waste of time and money since nobody hardly sees 'em anyways.
- To keep the sole stitchin' lookin' good, wash it fairly regular with a toothbrush and plain ol' soap and water.
- Keep your boots by the side of your bed if you smoke. If you drop your ashes into 'em, they'll stay smellin' fairly fresh. *Don't* keep your boots there if you dip or chew. Men has been knowed to confuse a boot with a spittoon in the dark.
- Never wear the same pair of boots two days in a row. You got to give 'em a chance to breathe.

THE WELL-DRESSED REDNECK: BODY COVERIN'S

BRITCHES

Movin' up a notch, we got to talk britches. For britches you might as well say jeans, and for jeans you might as well say Wranglers, Levis, or Lees. While they're alright for womenfolk, them designer jeans ain't worth a hoot for a man.

Far as the cut of the jean goes, the top two choices is cowboy cut, with a straight leg and a little extry fullness where a real man's got a little extry, and boot cut, with a slight flare to fit over boot tops easy. If you wear your britches' legs down inside your boot tops, straight legs is the best choice. We got to admit we don't think much of this style, but we'll set out the pros and cons of it for you anyway:

Pros
• Keeps the chiggers and ticks off of your legs if you're workin' in the woods.
• Keeps your britches from catchin' on barb wire or in workin' machinery.
• Keeps your britches bottoms clean if you're workin' in mud or around livestock.
• Keeps your britches from ridin' up between your leg and a horse's flank if you're ridin'.

Cons
• You can easy ruin the shank and stitchin' of your boot if it ain't covered by your britches.
• It's hard to keep both legs tucked in if you're movin' around at all, so you get a kinely lopsided, one in and one out, look to you.

We don't reckon the pros is all that pro; britches used for work is supposed to look like work britches. And it looks kinely sissified for a man to be all tucked in that-a-way.

SHIRTS

The western shirt fits better, feels better, and looks better than any other kind of shirt for lots of reasons:

- They got a tapered body so's they fit next to you like a second hide and don't go balloonin' out around your middle. Even if your middle goes balloonin' out on its own, you can still wear western shirts. They're cut slim, but not all *that* unpractical slim.
- They got longer tails to 'em on account of most folks a-wearin' 'em do a lot of movin' around workin' and playin'. This saves you from havin' your shirt untucked and sloppy lookin'.
- They got a yoke on the front and back for good looks. Sometimes the yoke is just set off by pipin' or top-stitchin', but on some it also is made of contrastin' material. These look real sharp.
- They got pearlized snaps rather than buttons on the front and the cuffs. Makes 'em easier and faster to shuck off for whatever reason you might have.

IT'S A CINCH: BELTS AND BUCKLES

While galluses (also called suspenders) is not *bad* to wear for keepin' your britches up, they ain't nearly as pretty as a well-made belt with a sharp-lookin' buckle on it.

Your *basic* redneck belt has got to be, no question about it, tooled leather with your name on the back and your initials on the tip. We heard tell that some folks been sayin' the reason rednecks put their names on their belts is so when they decide to pull their heads out of their rears, they'll know who they are. That ain't real funny. The main reason is so's folks never meet a stranger and can call newly met individuals by their name right off.

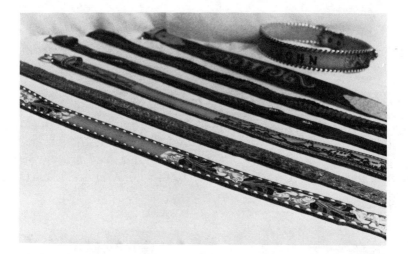

For fancy wear you can buy a belt made from one of the exotic leathers or hides that will match your fancy boots, or a variety of designs in plain ol' cowhide. A braided nylon belt, that looks kinely like horse riggin', is good for times between the workin' ones and the fancy dress ones.

Buckles ought to be as a big as a 'dozer blade and as shiny as a new dime up a goat's rear. Your basic buckle ought to have a western scene of some sort on it or your name or initial. Variations include:

- Ranger buckle with tip and keeper.
- Clear resin with somethin' inside it: spiders, scorpions, money, etc.
- Extry longs, which are worn on the side above the hip bone rather than right above the fly of your britches.

THE CROWNIN' GLORY: HATS

No man's complete without one, and most real rednecks have two: a felt for wintertime and a straw for the summer. The changeover times from one to the other are Easter, when you put on the straw, and Labor Day, when you break out the felt.

FELT FACTS

- The more the number of XXs you got in your felt, the better it is. Good workin' hats is "XXX Beaver"; fancier models go up to "XXXXXXXXXX Beaver." What this tells you is the amount of beaver hair mixed into the felt. The more beaver, the longer wear you get from the hat. A felt hat ought to last at least two or three years, less you're a fightin' man.
- Better hats come "open crown," which is with no crown crease, so a man can get the crease he wants steamed in by a professional hat shaper.
- The dip, which is how you shape the front and back of the rim, and the roll, which is how you shape the sides, is also a matter of personal choice. Dip and roll possibilities are:

Roper:	Front kinely flat; back turned up a mite; sides fairly straight
Rancher:	Slight dip front and back; side rolled
Bullrider:	Radical dip front and back; sides rolled to taste

STRAW STORY

- Don't usually last for more than one summer even if you *ain't* a fightin' man.
- Usually come preshaped, but a professional shaper can personalize your dip and roll a little.
- Not really worth lookin' at till it's got a sweat ring around the base of the crown.
- Panama's the best straw, with seaweed, hemp, sisal, and Bangora your other choices.

Hint: Don't never go to buy a new hat on Monday mornin'. That's when there's always a big run on 'em. Lots of hats get ruint in Saturday night fights or left in places where a man can't go back to fetch it.

HAT BANDS

Made out of most everything you can imagine. Most common seen are:

- feathers
- reptile skins
- braided horsehair
- beads

The real redneck always carries a little extry thing or two tucked into his hatband for looks and/or for usin':

- horseshoe nails
- toothpicks
- country and western concert ticket stubs (mostly for the younger set)
- peacock or guinea hen feathers

LITTLE EXTRIES: THE FINISHIN' TOUCHES

While it don't do to be gettin' too fancy most of the time, sometimes these little touches can set a man or a woman dressed to go out right off:

- Boot tacks. Mostly for womenfolk. These is little strips of jewels or other designs that you tap into your heel at the top of the back of it.
- Collar tips. Triangle-shaped silver or gold doodads that fasten on to the tip of both sides of your collar. Keeps 'em from flappin' or rollin' up and looks real fancy.
- Ties. Only, of course, ever now and then. You got three choices:

  Bolo tie—a thin, braided cord with a decoration (that's the bolo) that slides up and down and holds the two sides together. Bears a unsettlin' resemblance to a noose.
  String tie—a thin strip of material tied in a bow with some hang-down left over.
  Scarf tie—like it says, a long, thin scarf you knot around your neck.

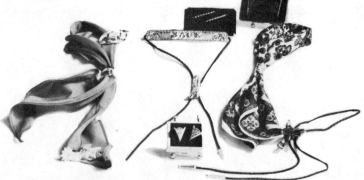

• Hat tacks. Little jewelry for your hat. There is a truckload of designs to choose from:

> Rodeo events
> Animals (hogs, bulls, armadillos)
> Snuff and beer cans
> Sayin's: "Rodeo Spoken Here," "You Touch My Hat, I'll Smash Your Face," etc.

MONOGRAMMIN'

This has become a big fashion idea in the last few years, and some of it's real works of art.

Men: Put your initials on your shirt pocket and/or sleeve cuff;
Put your name on the watch pocket of your dress jeans or on the bottom of your jean leg.

Women: Put your name and a fancy design on your back hip pocket and/or up the side of one of your britches' legs.

THEY IS ONE OF US:
REDNECK DESIGNER LINES

Although we don't hold much truck with folks who wear *other* folks names splashed across their rear ends, it ain't so bad when the name is at least American and belongs to a good ol' boy or gal who's as common as we are. Makes sense, too, that folks born and raised country got to know more about country clothes than a foreigner from New York City or even out of the U.S. of A. altogether. Closest most of *them* ever come to country is on some dude ranch, you can bet.

Some of the young 'uns who been influenced by TV and the large number of foreigners comin' to live in our part of the country have kinely strayed over to Calvin Klein and Ralph Lauren. While we're sure Cal and Ralph is both good ol' boys down deep inside, we can't help hopin' that the kids'll come to their senses soon. The followin' listed people know what they're doin' and their western clothes show it. If you got to go fancy, for the Lord's sake, go it with them.

- Larry Mahan. All around rodeo champ more times than you can shake a stick at.
- Dolly Parton. Even though Dolly has kinely expanded out past country, nobody expands out better than her. She's all woman and plenty of it, and she makes clothes that make a woman look like a woman even though very few of 'em look quite as *much* like a woman as she does.
- Mickey Gilley. Besides bein' one hell of a singer and piano player, Mickey owns the famous Gilley's Club in Pasadena, Texas. He knows what's necessary for dancin' ease in western clothes.
- Kenny Rogers. Another singer gone designer who knows what he's doin'.
- Willie Nelson. While Willie hisself don't always dress in nothin' more than the rattiest ol' tee-shirts and jeans, he's got his name on some fine lookin' shirts and such.

4

Fry a Little Tenderloin:
Eatin' and Cookin' Redneck Style

EATIN' IN

WE BEEN TALKIN' so far mostly about the outside things; now it's time to move innards. Rednecks got to eat just like anybody else, but what we eat ain't nothin' like what nobody else eats. If there's any truth to the idea that you are what you eat, we reckon it's better to be a big ol' piece of chicken-fried steak or peach cobbler than some ol' crab or lobster.

In our part of the country, eatin' is a simple thing. We figger that fancy foods cooked even fancier takes all the pleasures out of chowin' down. A man eats 'cause he's feelin' kinely narrow in the flanks, and it's bound to take good, solid food to fill him up proper.

What we got here is some suggestions on what to eat and how to cook it up right so's it'll taste the way it was meant to. This is plain ol' American food cooked the plain ol' American way. There just ain't nothin' better tastin' nor better for you.

CALLIN' YOUR MEALS RIGHT

Before you can plan and learn how to cook meals deservin' of the name of redneck, you got to learn to call the names of the meals straight. Rednecks eat three meals a day, and we generally don't miss a-one, neither. First meal of the day is breakfast, second is dinner, and third is supper. There ain't now nor has there ever been no such a thing as lunch. Therefore, it follows logical-like that folks who ain't home for dinner takes it with 'em in a dinner bucket. (We ain't never heard of a lunch box.) Anybody who eats dinner after two o'clock in the evenin' stood in bed too late that mornin'.

TEN IMPORTANT RULES TO FOLLOW IN COOKIN' AND EATIN'

1. Fry everythin'.
2. Use every part of everythin' you possibly can. In other words, don't waste nothin'.
3. Never toss out your grease. Keep a drippin's can on the cook stove to keep it in. If you don't want to buy one of the fancy models, an ol' coffee can will do fine. If your grease starts to take on a kinely funny taste after a spell (and if you've cooked up catfish it surely will do just that), cook a couple of pieces of raw potato in it for a few minutes. This'll absorb up the funny taste right quick.
4. Cook everything real done. Some folks like their meat so rare it darn near moos when they stick a fork to it. This ain't real good with beef, but it's plumb dangerous with pork and with home-canned vegetables.
5. Cook in cast iron pots and pans whenever possible. They soak up and give off flavorin'. Them little bits a iron that come off in the scrapin' part of cookin' is good for your red blood cells, too.
6. Never measure anything. Cookin' ain't no science; you ain't buildin' a piano when you're a-stirrin' up a meal.
7. Grow, shoot, or trap as much of what you eat as you can. First off, it'll taste better'n store-bought food. Second, there ain't no reason to pay good money out for what the Good Lord provides free to them that's got the gumption to go out and get it.
8. Never serve any meal without fried potatoes and plenty of bread or biscuits.
9. Always cook enough to feed at least four more than you got in your immediate family. It ain't no tellin' who might take a notion to drop by.

10. Invite anybody who drops by to stay and eat, be they kinfolk, friends, or just strangers a-passin' through. It ain't nothin' like a home-cooked meal to make strangers over into friends.

COMMON MENU FOR A COMMON DAY

Breakfast

Buttermilk Biscuits	Fried Potatoes
Cream Gravy	Preserves, Honey,
Fried Ham	Sorghum
Fried Eggs	Coffee and Milk

Dinner

Swamp Rabbit and	Fried Taters
Cream Gravy	Homemade Bread
Fried Okra	Ice Tea and Milk

Supper

Cornbread and Buttermilk or Sweet Milk

RECEIPTS AND COOKIN' INSTRUCTIONS

Breakfast

BUTTERMILK BISCUITS, CREAM GRAVY, FRIED EGGS, FRIED SAUSAGE, FRIED TATERS

Buttermilk Biscuits

Before you commence makin' these here soppin' tools, you might ought to get one thing straight: there ain't *no* shortenin' in 'em 'cause that works to make 'em light and flaky. They ain't *supposed* to be light and flaky. They is *supposed* to be solid so's they don't fall to pieces when you're usin' 'em to sop up the gravy *and* so's once they get where they're a-goin', you'll know they're there and that you can count on 'em a-stayin' there 'til dinner time.

Mix two cups of buttermilk with a pinch of salt, a pinch of bakin' soda, and a couple of teaspoons of bakin' powder. The bakin' powder raises 'em up just enough so's you don't end up with ol' flat tack biscuits. Stir this up real good. When the powder goes to work a-foamin' up, add your flour (about two and a half cups to begin with) and work it in real good with a long-handled spoon. Add what flour you need to make the dough firm but not stiff. Then dump the dough out on a floured board and work in enough more raw flour so's it all hangs together and you can pat it out to the thickness of a saddle blanket—about half to three-quarters of an inch. Don't overwork the dough 'cause that'll make your biscuits tough. Men are tough; biscuits are firm. Next, flour up the rim of your jelly glass and get to cuttin' 'em out. Put some warm meat drippin's in your bakin' tin, dip each biscuit in the drippin's on both sides, and bake 'em. You ought to start 'em out at about 425 degrees and cook 'em 'til they're the color of a young hick'ry nut.

Cream Gravy

With the drippin's you got left in the skillet from fryin' your ham after greasin' up your biscuit tin, you're a-goin' to make the cream gravy. Get this grease real hot and then stir in enough flour to make a kinely runny paste. Salt and pepper with a free hand, 'cause them little flecks of black pepper a-swimmin' around in the white gravy is a thing a beauty. Brown your flour for a few minutes, stirrin' all the time so's you don't scorch it. Pour in a couple a cups a milk and keep a-stirrin' to prevent any lumpin' from goin' on. The gravy will look kinely thin at this point, but as it cooks up, it'll thicken up. Keep a-cookin' and a-stirrin' until it surely has, 'cause it ain't no good if you got to chase it 'round the plate with your biscuit to sop it. Good cream gravy takes a shape. It stays where you put it, which ought to be on top of everything you got on your plate. You ought to put back at least one biscuit to sop up whatever falls off the eggs and meat and sticks to the plate.

As a sidenote, you ought to put back at least two more to cap off the meal with some sweetenin'. Don't never butter these endin' biscuits and then spread the sweetenin' on top. To do it redneck style, scoop out a pat or two a butter onto your plate and add the sweetenin' to it, whether it's honey, preserves, or sorghum. Mash the two up together good with your fork and pile the conglomeration on the biscuit.

MEAT AND EGGS

Fryin' up the meat and eggs don't take no special know-how. Just drop the meat in the skillet and brown it good. Fry the eggs in the drippin's before you make the gravy.

Dinner

SWAMP RABBIT, CREAM GRAVY, POKE SALAD, SMASHED TATERS, CORN PONE

Swamp Rabbit

Swamp rabbit is some of the best eatin' meat they are. A perfect-ready swamp rabbit—also called a blue-nose swamp—is a hair bigger'n a cottontail, along about the size of a full-growed tame rabbit. Swamps tend to live in dens in bottom land. A good shot can ping one with a .22, but those lackin' a real good eye and a steady hand might want to start out with a shotgun. Of course, if you do this second way, you got to be real careful in the cleanin' to get out all the pellets. *Nothin'* hurts worse than to chomp down hard on a piece a shot unexpected; it'll sure enough jar your kinfolks in Bow Legs, OK.

For those of you not real familiar with the ways of swamp, we got a handy hint for a-gettin' you one. Take yourself to a nice piece of bottom land and scout around for the swamp's droppin's. Swamps got a peculiar habit of a-crawlin' up on an ol' stump or felled log to do their business, so once you spot the sign you can just hunker down and wait for them to pop up in answer to nature's call.

Once you bagged him, skin him out and cut him up in fryin'-size pieces. Wash all the pieces real good, salt and pepper 'em to taste, and roll 'em in flour. Fry 'em in real hot grease 'til they're brown, just like you would chicken. Once the pieces are brown, turn down the fire, cover the fry pan, and steam fry 'em 'til they're tender and cooked through.

Fried Okra

Whiles your rabbit is a-fryin', you can tend to your taters and other vegetable. We highly recommend fried okra to fill this second spot. First thing you got to do in fryin' okra is to make sure you pick out the littlest pods 'cause they're the most tender. You can tell if a pod is too tough to mess with by just a-tryin' to cut into it. If it's too old, you ain't a-goin' to be able to do no more'n just make a scratch on the skin.

Next thing to do is wash all the pods real good to make certain you got rid of all the little fuzzy prickles on the outside. If you got sensitive hands, you might ought to wear

FRIED OKRA FIXIN'S: CORNMEAL, OKRA, PAPER SACK, SALT

gloves while you're a-cleanin' and for sure while you're a-pickin' 'em out a the garden, 'cause them fuzzies will get under your skin and start you itchin' up a storm. They don't hurt near's bad as the juice from fresh jalapeño peppers—that burns like a coal of fire—but they'll sure hurt enough to get your attention.

After you wash 'em, cut off the stem cap and the pointy end of each pod. Then slice what's left in pieces about one-quarter inch thick; they ought to kinely remind you of lug nuts about now. Put a cup or so of cornmeal in a paper sack and shake up the okra in it real thorough to coat each piece. Okra lets off a kinely slimy juice when it's cut into, so you don't have to worry none about the meal a-stickin'. Dump the mess into a skillet full of hot bacon grease and fry it over medium heat 'til it's brown and crispy on the outside and tender on the inside.

Note: Some folks prefer their okra boiled rather'n fried. It ain't real bad that way, but the slimy nature of this vegetable tends to make boiled okra kinely slide down your gullet without you a-havin' to help it along none. If this don't bother you, after the washin' just drop the whole pods into boilin', salted water and cook 'em til you can stab 'em with a fork without exertin' yourself none.

THE FINISHED PRODUCT

Bread

If you baked bread earlier in the day, you don't got to worry about gettin' your biscuits in the oven. We might suggest that you keep in mind that while home-baked bread is mighty handy to swaller, biscuits go best with any meal containin' cream gravy. Light bread, of course, is plumb out a the question. It may do for a Vienna sausage sandwich, but no real cook would ever serve it with dinner.

Finishin' Up

When the rabbit's fried, you make cream gravy in the pan drippin's just like you done at breakfast. Cream gravy's cream gravy no matter what meal you eat it at.

Supper

Dinner is most usually the big meal of the day for most folks considerin' themselfs redneck. Supper is generally a light meal, 'cause it don't do well to go to bed with a overloaded stomach. Dinner a-bein' served anywheres from 11:30 A.M. to 1:00 P.M.; the logical time for supper to begun bein' thought of is 6:00 or 6:30 P.M. That gives a body an hour or so most nights to digest it down good before turnin' in.

Cornbread and buttermilk is one of the best light suppers they are. If buttermilk don't set real easy with you, you can just as easy use sweet milk. All this involves is makin' up a pan of cornbread, lettin' it cool down for a few minutes, and crumblin' it up in fairly good-size pieces into a bowl of some sort. Those two pound oleo tubs are perfect for this. Pour the milk over the crumbled bread and let it soak up for a minute or two, then get after it. You may need to add a little more milk 'fore you're through, bein' as cornbread kinely acts like a sponge.

CORNBREAD 'N' BUTTERMILK

Note: If you've had brown beans and cornbread for dinner, you can cut out the cookin' step here altogether. Even if the leftover bread's a bit hard by supper time, it won't make no never mind. The milk'll soften it up good in no time.

ADDITIONAL RECEIPTS

What you're about to turn on to is a collection of possible substitutions for the dinner meal, rangin' from meat to vegetables. We've also gone on and throwed in a few specialty items, but we're serious as a heart attack when we tell y'all that you might ought to stick pretty close to meat, gravy, taters, and bread 'cause they're the food that'll stick close to you in turn.

Meat Substitute #1: Calf, Lamb, Turkey, or Pork Fries

We might as well get this over with right quick. That that's called "fries" is by their clinical name testicles. What we call 'em down home shouldn't ought to be no big mystery to no one. Lots of folk gets kinely a weak-stomached feelin' when introduced for the first time to the idea of actually eatin' fries. Tell them pantywaists what they're eatin', and you can bet the farm they'll be a-gaggin' and a-spittin' 'fore you can say doodly-squat. This type of person puts us in mind of the ol' boy who refused to eat beef tongue on account of it come from the mouth of a dirty ol' cow, but who wouldn't a missed his two eggs every mornin' for nothin' or nobody. Not that we're complainin', now. Seein's as fries got to come from a male animal and seein's as any given male animal can't spare no more than the two he's got, too big a run on these delicacies might make 'em plumb scarce.

You can buy fries in some grocery stores, but the store-bought ones can't hold the fresh ones a light. Come the spring of the year when ranchers cut their bull calves, there's lots of smilin', happy folks to be seen enjoyin' the hell out a these treats come straight from the source, which in this case is definitely *not* the horse's mouth.

We ain't botherin' to provide a picture of fries 'cause we figger when you seen two, you seen 'em all. Knowin' then what they look like, here's what you got to do to find out what they taste like.

To prepare fries for cookin', split the sac open and peel it off. Then just soak the meat in cold salt water for twelve hours or so to draw off all the blood and lessen what's otherwise a pretty stout taste. When you take the meat out of the water, wash it real good in cold fresh water; salt, pepper, and flour it just like you would any meat you was aimin' to fry; and brown it good in hot grease.

Note: Fries is best when they're sliced real thin before bein' coated in flour and cooked. It ain't a bad idea to put 'em in the freezer for a short while after you wash 'em to kinely firm 'em up enough to manage this. They're tough to keep a holt of when they ain't froze.

A Little Extry Note on Fries

We heard tell not too long ago of a good story concernin' this particular taste treat. Seems there was this ol' French boy who come to Oklahoma and got hisself a job on a workin' ranch. First day, come sunup, the foreman sent the ol' boy out to help the hands cut the new calf crop so as to make steers out a the bull calfs. Ol' Pierre, we'll call him, was a-cuttin' away to beat the band and a-tossin' what he cut off into the nearest ditch when the foreman come 'round to check on him. "What in hell are you a-doin'?" he hollered. "Don't throw them away. We fry 'em up and mortally devour them things, son. They're called 'calf fries.'"

Come next mornin', the foreman sent Pierre out again; this time to help cut the sheep herd. When the foreman come 'round again to check up on him later, there was ol' Pierre a-cuttin' and a-tossin' all over again. The foreman crawled his frame worse'n he had the day before. They heard him in three counties as he shouted, "I thought I tole you to save them things, boy. We fry up and eat these same's we do calf fries, only these are called 'lamb fries.' Just to keep the record straight, we do the same with turkey and call 'em 'turkey fries,' and with boar hog and call 'em 'pork fries.' You think you got that, now?"

The next mornin', the foreman sent Pierre out where he couldn't do no serious damage. He set him to diggin' post holes whilst the rest a the hands finished up the cuttin'. Around dinner time he went a-lookin' for Pierre, but couldn't find him nowheres. He finally wandered into the kitchen and asked the cook if he'd seed ol' Pierre. "Sure did," said the cook, "and them furriners is plumb strange. He come in here a while back and ast me what we was a-havin' for dinner, and when I told him he lit out a here like a horse with a burr under his saddle blanket." "Well, if that don't beat everything I ever slept with," said the foreman. "What in hell'd you tell him we was a-havin'?" "Guess he ain't much on American food," answered the cook, "'cause all we're a-havin' is hamburgers and french fries."

Meat Substitute #2: Chicken-Fried Steak

While we ain't got nothin' against a nice, thick sirloin or a T-bone charcoaled to perfection, there ain't nothin' that'll beat a nice piece of round steak chicken-fried right brown. Pan-fryin' steak's got the added advantage of gravy drippin's, of course, and that's reason enough for us to favor it over grill-cookin'. It's tough to catch enough drippin's for gravy when you cook outside, and dinner without gravy is like a man without his hat. It just don't seem finished off, somehow.

There's kinely a on-goin' debate over the best way to cook chicken-fried steak. Some folks, who we got to say we think of as close to lazy, make up a batter of flour, egg, and milk, and just dip the meat into this conglomeration. Mama *never* did it that-a-way, though, and we don't recommend it for you on the strength of that fact. Everybody's always a-lookin' for a shortcut to save a step or two. Well, what you gain in time a-usin' the batter method you sure lose in flavor. Batter *ain't* better.

CHICKEN-FRIED STEAK, CREAM GRAVY,
SMASHED TATERS, FRIED OKRA,
BISCUITS

The right way to make chicken-fried steak is to put your flour on one plate and mix up your eggs and a drop of milk in a separate dish. First step is to salt and pepper the meat and place it in the flour, turnin' it to coat both sides. The next step is the most important, and the one you miss usin' the batter method. Take the flour coated meat and hit it a few good licks with the side-edge of a heavy saucer on each side. This kinely pounds the flour into the meat while at the same time tenderizin' the steak. *Then* you dip the meat into the egg-and-milk mix and slap it back into the flour for a second go-round. You can kinely think of the first trip as layin' on the primer coat and the second as the finish coat.

Get your grease real hot, hot enough to make a few sprinkles of flour hop around like a barefooted feller in a field full of cockleburs, and ease the pieces of meat down into it. Cook it all the way brown on the first side before turnin' it to cook on the second. If you go to turnin' it over and over, you'll sure enough knock the coatin' off and end up with plain ol' pan-fried steak. It ain't a good idea to cover the pan while the steak's a-cookin', neither. The steam will cause the coatin' to kinely lift right off the meat. No sense a-goin' to all the fuss of preparin' the meat right before you fry it if you're a-goin' to lose all the coatin' while you're a-fryin' it, now, is there?

Common Meat Substitutes #3–#9

Other meats to fry up for dinner are, of course, chicken and pork chops. Then there's always turkey breast, which most folks don't know tastes better'n chicken when it's rolled in flour and fried. Also of course, if you've flushed up a covey of quail, jumped a cottontail, or stirred up a squirrel in the mornin', any one of them is fittin' cleaned, cut up, rolled in flour, and fried.

Deer meat, which some folks go to the trouble of callin' venison, can be better'n beef if the deer's got in the right area and dressed right directly after it's killed. Best way to do the steaks is to chicken-fry 'em just like you would beef steak. Meat that you don't cut up in steaks is best ground up coarse and used along with your pork when you're makin' your own sausage, or mixed with ground beef and pork for chili.

Gravy Substitute: Red-Eye

Hard as it is to imagine, ever now and then a body can get tired of cream gravy. This don't happen very often, but when it does there's a substitute that ain't half bad: red-eye gravy. You can only make red-eye when you fried ham or bacon. All you do is add brewed coffee to the hot grease, stir it up good until it comes to a rollin' boil, and set to it. You got to eat this real fast, 'cause while cream gravy'll kinely set up to soft cement consistency as it cools down, red-eye will plumb congeal bein' as how it's nothin' much more'n coffeed-down grease to begin with.

Vegetable Substitute: Greens, All of 'Em but 'Specially Poke

Mustard and turnip greens boiled down with bacon grease for seasonin' goes with just about any meat dish. Mustard greens is also fittin' cooked down with a few shots of tabasco sauce and garlic salt. The best greens they are, though, is poke, also called poke salad. Come spring of the year, anybody with any gumption about him can gather up enough poke to do for an entire year. Canned or put up in the deep freeze, poke stays delicious. Gatherin' up poke don't take hardly no time or effort, though bein' as it boils down consid-

UNCOOKED GREENS AND FIXIN'S

erable you got to gather two or three peck sacks full to make a mess.

Poke grows the most thick 'round ol' brush piles, so if a man's done some 'dozin' on his place to clear it and left some of the piles unburned, you're in for easy pickin's. Watch out for snakes, though. They like them ol' brush piles almost as much as poke does.

Main thing to remember in pickin' poke is to take off only the top leaves, 'cause they're the youngest and tenderest. You can cook the stalks and all of the very tops of the plants. Just wash 'em four or five times to make sure you got the grit off, put 'em in a big pot with a little water, and get 'em to boilin'.

Some folks swear that the water you boil the poke in is poisonous as a copperhead, so they boil it down for a spell, pour off the first water, and finish the cookin' in fresh. There's others, though, say that drunk straight off, this first water will do everything from releasin' you if your bowels are bound up to curin' arthritis. In a cure or kill situation like this one, we like to be on the safe side. So, 'til there's more definite information on this here matter, we recommend a-pourin' off the first water and not takin' no unnecessary chances. Growin' old a-sufferin' with arthritis ain't so good, but the alternative's a darn sight worse.

Only seasonin' you need for poke is a couple a big globs a

COOKED GREENS

bacon grease or slabs a fat back and salt. Simmer the poke 'til it's real soft and tender. The longer you cook it, the better it is. Best advice to keep in mind a-cookin' any kind of greens is the story about the ol' boy who was asked the best way to cook kidneys. "It ain't nothin' to it," he told the asker. "Just toss 'em in a pot of water and boil the piss out of 'em."

VARIATIONS

1. A good light supper comes from scramblin' up a bunch of eggs with cooked poke.
2. You can also cook poke stalk like you would okra. Slice it up in little rounds, coat it in cornmeal, and fry it. You still need to stay kinely near the top of the plant, though, 'cause the bottom of the stalk is as tough as that ol' rooster the ol' gal boiled up for chicken and dumplin's. She claimed she boiled it hard for three days and three nights and couldn't even stick a fork in the broth.

Whole Meal Substitute #1: Catfish and Go-Withs

Once you got aholt of a mess of fresh catfish, cleaned, fileted, and soaked in a bucket a salt water overnight, you are on your way to a dinner that won't don't. Be sure to soak the fish, 'cause you need to draw out all the blood to end up with what catfish ought to be: the whitest, prettiest meat you ever did see. If you ain't a-goin' to eat 'em right off, you can put 'em up in the deep freeze. Don't just bag 'em and drop 'em in, though. They'll sure enough get that ol' freezer taste if you do. Instead, freeze 'em in water in one of them half-a-gallon milk cartons. If they're froze in water this-a-way, they'll taste like they just come from the lake when you finally thaw 'em out and cook 'em up.

THE ACTUAL COOKIN'

Dump a few handfuls of cornmeal into a paper sack and then throw in the salted and peppered strips of fish. Shake 'er up good, then drop the pieces into the hot grease.

The best way to cook cat is outside over a hot wood fire in a cast iron pot. Not only will your fish taste better this way, but you'll feel better not havin' to be a-listenin' to the wife's fussin' about your dirty ol' fish a-stinkin' up her whole house.

The key to success here is that the grease has got to be rollin', larrupin' hot. If it ain't, your fish will just go to soakin' it up like a sponge. When the grease is at a gallopin' boil, drop in the first mess. They'll sink right to the bottom of the pot, but don't pay that no mind. Soon as they start gettin' done, they'll come a-floatin' to the top and start a-bobbin' 'round like the head of an ol' boy smack in the middle of a three-day runnin' drunk. When they do, scoop 'em out and drain 'em good before eatin'.

Note: If you got any fondness at all for the hair on your hands and lower forearms, you'd best be for makin' yourself a long-handled scoop out of an old dipper or saucepan. Just punch a few drain holes in the bottom and you'll have a strainer that'll allow you to keep a safe distance from the fire.

Go-Withs

The only fittin' go-withs for catfish is hush puppies and cole slaw. The slaw ought to be made the night before so's it can sit in the icebox overnight and get right. Cook your hush puppies after you cook your fish. They only take a minute or two, and if you don't eat 'em right off out a the pot, they lean toward gettin' kinely soggy and tough.

Hush Puppies

To build the hush puppies you just mix up a batch of cornbread, cuttin' down on the milk a little so's you can roll the batter up into little balls that'll stay little balls while they're a-cookin'. Plain ol' puppies ain't nothin' to sneer at, but doctorin' 'em up with some chopped onion and jalapeño peppers will make 'em taste so good they'll make you want to slap your granny.

A word a caution about dealin' with fresh jalapeños is necessary here. Don't touch 'em. If the juice gets into your skin, you'll be a-lookin' for a place to get off, and quick. That ol' stuff burns like you ain't never felt nothin' but pure fire burn. There ain't no cure for it, neither. You can spray your hands with store-bought burn medicine, rub 'em with butter, and pack 'em in ice 'til the cows come home, but your ol' grabbers will never know you done one thing to help 'em out in the least way. We've seed full-growed men that's got callouses big as Dallas and thick as a woman's head on their hands, a-sittin' with tears as big as horse turds just a-streamin' down their cheeks on the strength of this a-happenin' to 'em. Either use rubber gloves or stab them things with a fork while you're a-cuttin' 'em up to avoid any physical contact whatsoever. Along the same lines, you might ought to cut 'em up real fine. Friends who bite into too big a chunk may not remain friends too long. You'd be a-wastin' the fish, too, 'cause after one of them peppers gets done with the inside of your mouth, your ol' taste buds is plumb numb 'til come-next-tater-diggin'.

Whole Meal Substitute #2: Brown Beans and Ham Hocks with Cornbread

While most of us rednecks is proud to call ourselfs meat and taters men, down deep we're always more'n willin' to pass both up for a big ol' plate a brown beans and ham hocks restin' atop about a yard and a half of cornbread. We been told that ol' Will Rogers once had packed away a major portion of a pot a beans when his wife offered him a big slice of homemade apple pie for dessert. Bein' the smart feller he was, Will told her straight off that if he could find room anywheres for that piece of pie, he'd darn sure have had another plate of beans.

Fixin' up a pot of beans involves some necessary preparations. First, you got to spread your dried beans out on a flat surface so's you can pick out the bad 'uns and any little rocks that made it into the bin or bag, dependin' on whether you bought 'em in bulk or prepacked. Bitin' into a rock whilst you're a-chewin' your beans is as bad as bitin' into a piece a shot in rabbit or squirrel. You could even break a tooth and put the hurt on your eatin' activities for a spell.

Once you got 'em picked over careful, scoop 'em into your pan and wash 'em good, pourin' off at least three panfulls of wash water to make sure you got out all the dirt.

To cook 'em, you can, of course, like in everything else, either take the fast and easy way or do it right. The fast and easy way is to put your beans, hocks, and some salt in your pressure cooker, rev it up to fifteen pounds and cook it for about forty-five minutes. The right way is to fill the pan with water once again and let those brown beauties soak for four or five hours. Then pour off the final soakin' water and cover 'em with fresh. Add salt and the hocks, put 'em on medium fire, and cook 'em 'til they're real tender.

Best way to eat these once they're done good is to split open your cornbread on a plate and spoon plenty of beans, hocks, and juice all over it. Now that'll toot your horn.

SNACKS AND THE DINNER BUCKET

Nothin' aggravates us more than a home where real cookin' don't go on almost constant. All them prepackaged foods is priced plumb out of reason, full of chemicals we wouldn't spray on skeeters, and lackin' one important thing: good taste. Sometimes, though, given the fast pace of life nowadays, a man's got to settle for somethin' less than home-cooked for a quick snack or for a totable to carry in his dinner bucket. Broke down into logical categories, the ones listed out below will do:

CANDY

GooGoo Clusters—Anything advertised on the Grand Ol' Opry couldn't be all bad.

Peanut Patties—These are also called Peanut Rounders in some parts of the country.

OTHER SWEETS

Fried Pies—Not anywhere's near Mama's real thing, but the peach ones are eatable.

Sandwich Meats

Spam—Two slices fit on one piece of light bread perfect. Also comes in a paste for easy spreadin'.

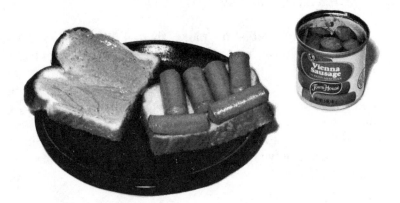

Vienna Sausages (pronounced Vy-āna)—Make sure you split 'em lengthwise so's they don't go a-rollin' off in your dinner bucket.

Pop

Mountain Dew
Dr. Pepper

EATIN' OUT

Eatin' out is kinely like workin' for wages; real rednecks try to avoid both whenever possible. First off, if a man's got a wife who can make any kind of a hand in the kitchen, he's bound to have better food to home than in some priced-plumb-out-of-reason restaurant. Second off, good digestion comes when a man's relaxed and at his ease. That feelin' is more likely to come on a man when he's in his own home where he can kick off his boots, loosen up his belt, and take off his shirt. All them

NO SHOES . . . NO SHIRT . . . NO SERVICE

signs plastered acrost the doors of restaurants is a good in-dication of the attitude they expect a man to have and act on. With all them restrictions, it ain't no way his food can relax and spread out over his body right to nourish it.

The final good reason for eatin' in rather'n out is a small one, but it's the kind of small like a speck a dust in your eye. Many of the supposed best restaurants don't even put tooth-picks on the table in easy reach. A sliver of meat in a man's teeth can drive him plumb crazy and come close to spoilin' his eatin'. Everybody knows to keep a spare or two tucked into their hatband, but in some of them high dollar places they even frown on a man wearin' his hat to the table.

Of course, a man's got to keep in mind that for some rea-son womenfolk like it real fine when they're took out to eat. To keep things a-runnin' smooth at the house, a man might ought to force his ol' self to take the poor overworked thing out ever now and then. Holidays is the likeliest time for these little excursions, but only if your kin ain't able to come so's y'all can be together on the occasion. If you ain't fortunate enough to have a lot of kin livin' close or, the Good Lord forbid, if you ain't got much, you can kinely plan on holidays and thank your lucky stars there ain't that many of 'em.

There ain't but three acceptable possibilities for places to eat. In order of plainest to fanciest, they are: drive-ins, cafes, and buffets at them big motels.

DRIVE-INS

One of the main advantages of drive-ins is said real plain in the story about the ol' boy who told his new gal friend, "This won't take long, honey, did it?" Don't let the speed advantage steer you wrong, though. If you're a-goin' to a drive-in, don't settle for a drive-through. They may be faster, but there's a limit to what a man can put down hisself even in the interest of gettin' done and gettin' home.

The best rule of thumb in choosin' a drive-in burger joint is this: the best has got to look the worst on the outside. You can just about figger that the money spent on needless arches and kiddie playgrounds ain't been spent on the most important thing: the meat that makes the burger.

Once the car hop brings you the burger you ordered, you can tell before even bitin' into it whether you've chose a good drive-in. Lookin' at the top of the bun, you ought to almost be able to see yourself in it. There ought to be a thin coatin' of grease on it resultin' from the cook havin' kinely mashed it down on the grill with the egg turner. Openin' up the bun and inspectin' the patty itself, you ought to discover that it's all lopsided and ragged around the edges, showin' that the cook made it up hisself and didn't just reach into a deep freeze and peel it off a stack of preshaped, bought ones. Most important, it ought to be brown, without the slightest tinge of gray. If it

DRIVE-IN GOODIES: BURGER, ONION RINGS, CHOCOLATE MALT

leans at all toward that color of woman's eye paint they call "taupe," you know you are fixin' to bite into soy, boy, and that's enough to drive any man to the sauce.

The third and final test comes in the actual eatin'. Taste excluded, the best way to determine a real hamburger is the number a times you got to put it down and wipe your forearm and elbows clean from runnin' grease. French fries is kinely the same way. While you don't want 'em to be like that new chewin' gum with the squirt in the middle, you don't want dry, baked taters either. If you prefer onion rings to fries, shape is the key to whether they're real or not. If they look like them kid's games consistin' of a series of regular, small rings that get throwed over a stick, they ain't. If they're kinely free-form, they are. A malt and/or a Dr. Pepper ought to finish you off pretty good.

Keep in mind two things about drive-ins that recommend 'em highly. First, sittin' in your truck a-eatin' is next best to sittin' in your own kitchen. Second, you're guaranteed a toothpick, 'cause they got to use one to hold the wrappin' paper around the burger.

Other Items on the Drive-In Menu to Consider

Corn Dogs: A distant cousin of the hot dog. Kinely a chicken-fried hot dog, really. Handy 'cause they come on a stick; unhandy 'cause the stick's too big to use as a toothpick. Watch out for the roof a your mouth the last few bites. Them sticks is pointed.

Chili Pies: A good-size handful of corn chips in one a them paper boats that looks like a party hat. Lots a chili spooned up into a hill on top of 'em and chopped onions thick as hail after a hail storm. Shredded cheese a-meltin' all over the top and a-drippin' down the side a the boat. The corn chips ought to get soggy and bright orange from the grease from the chili.

Brown Derby Cones: Soft ice cream dipped into hot chocolate syrup that gets brittle and hard real fast. Eat fast and never wear white when suckin' one down. Once you bite off the little curly-Q at the top, things start to get rough. Leaks from between the chocolate shell and the top of the cone, and chunks a fallin' chocolate is to be expected comin' pretty regular.

CAFES

There's a story 'bout an ol' boy who wanders into a local cafe who's done had a cravin' flung on him for a cup of coffee and a piece of pie. Sittin' down at the counter he sees right off the pie he wants restin' uncut on the counter directly in front of him. "I'll have a cup of coffee and a piece of that raisin pie," he tells the waitress. She looks at him, grabs a fly swatter, swings it real sharp a couple of times, and says, "Right away, sir, but this here's egg custard."

Now while you prob'ly don't want to find a cafe quite this rustic, you want to steer clear of the other extreme, too. Any place busy puttin' on the dog ain't a-goin' to have interest much in puttin' on a feed bag much to speak of. Clean, but simple and common is the best. Just like with drive-ins you can figger that if the food's good, they ain't a-goin' to worry none 'bout distractin' you from it with fancy trimmin' and such.

Signs for Trackin' Down a Good Cafe

- The vinyl booths ought to outnumber the formica dinette set tables and chairs by at least two to one.
- Food is served on melmac plates, and water and ice tea in them bumpy plastic glasses, either brownish gold or red.
- Toothpicks are on the table right between the salt and pepper shakers. They are *not* individually wrapped up in that white paper that gets wet and sticks to everything. They can be in an ol' shot glass, but they ought to be in one of them spice jars you get at the store that's got a plastic lid on it so's you can shake out your own through one of the holes.

TYPICAL CAFE MENU

- The menu has a plastic cover on it so's the grease can be wiped off rather'n soakin' into the paper so's you can't read what choices you got. The menu should also have one or more of them little metal clips at the top that allow for a "Daily Special" card to be tucked in.
- Each booth's got an individual jukebox so's you can be a-listenin' to music while you're a-chewin' without havin' to be gettin' up and goin' to the main juke box ever few minutes.

BUFFETS

These all-you-can-eat places is usually found in your fancier motels. While the food ain't usually as close to tastin' home-cooked as it is at a good cafe, it's generally fit to eat. The womenfolk like it 'cause they can wear their best pantsuit in and make you to put on a clean shirt and dress jeans and to polish your boots.

What's best about buffets, of course, is you can eat all you think you're big enough to. In other words, you can always make up in quantity what you may not get in quality. What's worst is that if you really get solid 'bout gettin' your money's worth, you could end up a-founderin' yourself. For them of you that don't know it, a horse is foundered when he eats too much. This causes his ol' hoofs to swell up and gets him a high fever. Unless he's took care of real quick and right, he could be ruint for life. If you got a wife who ain't big on eatin' or's on

one a them never-endin' diets they go on, you could be in a heap a hurt. You got to control yourself so's you won't be compelled to eat her money's worth, too.

Choices at a Good Buffet

SALADS

Pickled Beets
Corn Relish
Pickled Okra
Jalapeño Cheese Chunks
Spiced Apples
Iceberg Lettuce
Canned Peaches
Angel Fluff
   (Whipped toppin' with canned fruit, coconut, and nuts)
Jell-O Salad
   (Lime Jell-O with cottage cheese and nuts)
Black-Eyed Pea Salad
Three Bean Salad

SALAD FIXIN'S AT A BUFFET

Meats

Fried Chicken
Smoked Pork Chops
Chicken and Dumplin's
Chicken-Fried Steak Patties

MEATS

Gravy

Cream Gravy
Brown Gravy

Bread

Biscuits
Dinner Rolls

Vegetables

Mashed Potatoes
Hominy Grits
Green Beans With Bacon Bits
Cream Corn With Jalapeño Peppers

Dessert

Gooseberry Cobbler
Custard Pie

5

Mobile Home, Sweet Mobile Home: Housin' Redneck Style

A MAN'S HOME is his castle they say, and they darn sure got that right 'cause nowadays a man's got to be rich as a king to afford one. Lucky for us there is a alternative: the trailer house. In addition to not bein' priced plumb out of reason so's a workin' man can afford one, trailer houses is good livin' places for a couple of other reasons, too.

First, you can, if you buy a new one, get it already done up with furniture if you've a mind to. This cuts way down on the choicin' folks got to go through in riggin' out a home. All you got to do to make a trailer house your mobile home sweet mobile home is to let the little woman add some personal

belongin's to finish it out. Second, trailer houses move with you when you got to. Since a man never knows when he'll turn his land green and move off to a new location, this characteristic can come in mighty handy.

Although the way folks decorate their home is a personal matter, we're a-givin' out some suggestions for the ideal:

INSIDE

LIVIN' ROOM

Naugahyde couch with color-keyed crushed velvet recliner (broken).

TV trays.

Anything early American.

TV: rabbit ears with tin foil on for better reception; pliers on top of set to change channels.

Shag carpet: preferably olive green or harvest gold.

Fireplace with fake logs—buck head mounted above.

Animal skin rug in front of fireplace.

On mantle: horse (bronze color) with clock in belly (won at last county fair).

Fake knotty pine panelling.

Various velvet paintings: herd of horses, bullfighter, rodeo clown, etc.

Souvenir ashtrays.

State of Oklahoma, Texas, Arkansas, etc. placemats on plastic wood coffee table

Magazine rack with: *Argosy, VFW* and *Elks Club Newsletters,*
   True Detective, True Confessions, Soap Opera Digest,
   Reader's Digest, The Star, National Enquirer, Field and
   Stream.
Bookcase with full set of *Reader's Digest Condensed Books, The*
   Living Bible, Supermarket Encyclopedia.
Chair made from old tractor seat.
Lighted gun cabinet.
Record player with inspirational records, Billy Graham choir, Oral
   Roberts, Mantovani, Slim Whitman, TV Record Collection of-
   fers, 46 Country Hits (not sung by original artists), various
   country albums.

KITCHEN

TV on counter top.
Oscillating fan, one blade missing.
Leather-look formica on bar that divides livin' room from kitchen.
Vinyl bar stools.
Mason jars, jelly glasses, and full set of Levi Garret Snuff glasses
   for drinkin.
Melmac dishes in aqua and green floral pattern.
Drippin' can or old coffee can on stove for savin' grease.
Broken window mended with cardboard and duct tape.
Toothpick holder shaped like miniature brass spittoon.
Cream pitcher shaped like cow.
Bar of Lava soap or can of "Goop" on window sill with ripening
   tomatoes (in season) from the garden.

Dish towels made from flour sacks.

Old pressure cooker under sink for drips.

Newspaper in corner with old hubcap for dog's food and saucepan without handle for water.

Decorator pot holders/hot pads crocheted to look like overalls, sundresses, clusters of grapes, or the underpants of boys and girls.

MASTER BEDROOM

Color scheme: red and black.

Elvis Presley mirror.

Crushed velvet bedspread.

TV.

Stuffed animals/dolls from county fair.

Red flocked wall paper.

Gold-veined mirror tiles on one wall.

Night stand with pistol (a man's got to protect his home).

Boot jack.

Window-unit air conditioner.

Covered-wagon lamp.

Twelve months of the year china dolls.

Leather saddle.

Rodeo trophies.

BATHROOM

Matching set hand-crocheted tissue-box cover and toilet-tissue cover (doll with toilet paper under skirt).

Lucite toilet seat with barbed wire samples in it (available at Shepler's, I promise).

Marble-look formica on vanity.

Full set of Avon after-shave bottles along with a bottle of Redneck After Shave.

Shower curtain with western scene on it.

Gas wall stove.

Towels that come free in laundry detergent boxes.

Plaster-of-paris ducks or fish on the wall.

"Rules of the John" plaque.

OUTSIDE

CAR PORT

Green corrugated fiberglass roof with decorator wrought-iron supports.

Old washer and dryer.

Old refrigerator.

FRONT PORCH

Floor and steps covered with Astroturf.
Doormat with "Y'all come" or "Howdy" on it.
Old bench-seat from pickup for visitin'.

FRONT YARD

Doe and fawn on lawn.
Waterfall with cowboy on top.
Mailbox supported by old plow or old cream separator or rigid
    chain.
Trees painted white half-way up trunk to keep the ticks and other
    bugs off.

BACK YARD

Fifty-gallon drum converted to a BBQ.
Assorted old plumbing fixtures
Old john as a planter
Clothes line.
Chain hoist between two trees with motor out of old car.
Hog pen.
Garden.
Assorted stuff that might come in handy some day.
Horse trailer.

MAKIN' YOUR TRAILER HOUSE MORE SOLID

The only real drawback to livin' in a trailer house is livin' in one in twister country. If you live where the wind comes twistin' down the plain, you could be in a heap of hurt come spring and fall of the year. These acts of God ain't near as excitin' and fun as *The Wizard of Oz* makes 'em out to be. Rather than countin' on wakin' up after a twister to find a bunch of cute, short folk a-dancin' and a-singin', if you're livin' in a trailer house you might ought to count on not wakin' up at all.

Some folks depend only on tie-downs to secure their trailers. These is just heavy cables you attach to the mobile home and then stake in the ground on the other end. Others go so far as to brick in the trailer, makin' it look like a real house just *shaped* like a trailer house. Course, makin' your mobile home more solid this last way kinely turns it into a immobile home, but you can't have everything.

Note: If you think we're over-exaggeratin' the dangers of twisters to mobile home dwellers, just take a gander at the grocery store sacks used durin' the season. They tell you plain as day to get out of your trailer and into the nearest ditch if one's a-comin'. If you can't read or won't leave the comfort of your trailer house durin' a twister producin' storm, we suggest you use the bag for coverin' up your head and start prayin' real hard.

TWISTER WARNIN' GROCERY BAG

6

I Love My Truck:
Travelin' Redneck Style

WHILE A PICKUP ain't no horse, it's the closest thing to it nowadays. Kissin' your truck ain't quite as satisfyin' as kissin' your horse, but a modern redneck's got to face up to the realities of life.

Since you got to have a vehicle, you might as well have one that'll work for you, and that's what a truck will do. Unlike more flighty things like women and jobs, a pickup, treated with some respect and took care of proper, will be there when you need it. It's got to be said, too, that a truck's got it all over a horse in one way, and that's in totin' capability. Of course, there's no comparin' a pickup to one of those pregnant scooters that folks up north call cars. Them is fine when the little woman goes high-bobbin' around town, but it's no way for a busy man to get 'round in. Anybody ever tried feedin' cattle in the winter from the back a one of them cars knows what we mean.

FANCY RIGS

It's real nice to have a truck a man's proud of when he's a-drivin' the family out for supper at a drive-in or cafe, or when he's a-haulin' the kids and their friends to the gym for a ball game. But, an ol' truck that's too slick ain't worth a darn when it comes to useability. A truck's like a man; a few wrinkles and dents spread around testifies to character and experience. Just like a man, too, a pickup ought to have several items right up front 'cause you never know when you may need 'em.

The followin' shows pretty good what the perfect usin' truck ought to have inside and out:

INSIDE

Gun rack with shotgun and whip.
Hat rack to hold the hat while a man's drivin', i.e., don't crush my crown.
Decorative screen on rear window; for example, a rodeo scene, migrating ducks or geese, stampeding horses, or an armadillo.
Styrofoam cup on dash to spit in for those who (and there ain't many who don't) chew or dip. No carpet for those who prefer the floor to the cup.

IN BED OF TRUCK

Bale of hay.
Several empty oil cans.
Farm jack and no spare.
Balin' wire (you can fix anything with it).
Fence cutters—if you shoot a rabbit or a squirrel from the truck you got to git in to git it.
A hound.
Couple of chairs for the kids to sit in.

OUTSIDE

Ball trailer hitch for the horse trailer.
Mud flaps.
Running boards.
Side rails.
Running lights.

CARE AND WASHIN' INSTRUCTIONS

Best rule of thumb is don't much. It ain't hardly worth a man's trouble and time to keep an ol' workin' pickup too clean. You can plumb wear it out a-washin' it. On the other hand, there ain't no excuse for lettin' it get plumb ruint either, so a hose down ever now and then is recommended. We've seen some pickups look like the birds is a-plannin' to buy 'em, judgin' from the number of deposits they've made. If you got a second truck for goin' places in, you might ought to wash it fairly regular. It reflects on you kinely like her home does a woman.

SOME FITTIN' BUMPER STICKERS

There's an ol' joke says that "bump 'er" and "stick 'er" is the two steps in first meetin' up with an ol' gal and then completin' the meetin' with what will make her yours for life. We ain't arguin' the point, but the two words also work to-gether to name a object that helps a man make a statement about who he is and what he believes. There's a-plenty to choose from, but the ones listed out below will do just fine for lettin' folks know the driver of the vehicle they're decoratin' is redneck and proud of it.

"Cowboy Power"
"I'm Oil Field Trash and Proud of It"
"Redneck is Right"
"Pass at Your Own Risk. Driver Chews Tobacco"
"Please Don't Tell My Mama and Daddy I Work in the Oil
    Patch. They Think I'm a Piano Player in a Cat House"
"Control Commies, Not Guns"
"Coon Hunters Do It in the Woods"
"Yankees Go Home"
"People Who Want to Outlaw Guns Ought to be Shot"

7

Payin' the Rent and Havin' Some Fun: Workin' and Playin' Redneck Style

PAYIN' THE RENT: WORKIN' OUT IS A POOR WAY TO SERVE THE LORD

WORKIN' OUT, that is workin' for somebody else for wages, is one of the worst possible things we can think of. Most of us rednecks would sooner get out and scratch with the chickens than hire out. Wives, of course, tend to buck a little when a man don't have a steady job, what with the extry benefits of insurance, retirement, paychecks and all. But if a man's got any gumption about him, he can make enough just doin' around to get by. And gettin' by is really all a man needs to do. Any more'n that and he might get plumb spoilt. We feel about this kinely like the ol' boy who was asked how he liked his new trailer house. "Like it fine," he replied. "But then, never was used to too darn much, anyways."

If a man's got any management to him, he can make a good livin' tradin' and even manage to put some away for when he's too old to do much anymore. There's a-plenty out there to be done by a man with half an eye out and half a mind to. Lookin' for things he can buy worth the cap and then turnin' 'em green, a man can make enough to pay the bills at least. He can take up the slack in any number of ways, which we'll talk on after we're done with tradin'.

TRADIN': "WHAT YOU RECKON AN OL' THING LIKE THAT'S WORTH, ANYWAYS?"

Right off you got to be prepared for the fact that this way of makin' a livin' is goin' to lead to a domestic brawl or two, seein's as how to do it right a man's got to invest in some items that don't turn over real quick. And when the slow-turners has got to be stored in the yard, wives get to thinkin' of 'em as clutter rather'n inventory. But one woman's clutter is another man's fortune, so tune her out and pile it up.

One of the major pluses of tradin' is that a man don't generally have to over-exert himself goin' out and lookin' for some items to trade on. If you'll just put yourself in some locations where the ol' boys gather to jack their jaws, some ol' boy will sure enough come along with somethin' in the back of his pickup that he'll sell or trade.

STARTIN' HINTS

- Don't never look too interested or act too eager.
- Don't be in no all-fired hurry to get the trade done. Tradin' is kinely like makin' love. You got a better chance of gettin' done what you want if you don't get in no mad rush right out of the gates.

SLOW-TURNERS USUALLY GET STORED IN THE YARD

Startin'

Best way to get things goin' after you seen an item you'd
like to add to your inventory is to avoid even mentionin' it for
a spell. Ask the ol' boy who's got the thing you want about his
kids, the wife, his health, and so on. Then, when you got a
friendly atmosphere created, kinely look off in the distance,
spit a time or two, and ask: "Fair question, what'd you have
to give for that ol' ——— you got in your pickup?"

It ain't, of course, a fair question, and he ain't, of course,
goin' to tell you. But, you done sent out the signal that you're
ready to get solid and trade.

Your best next step is to commence some *serious* fishin' by
rephrasin' your question to: "Reckon what an ol' thing like
that's worth, anyways?" Now if you're dealin' with a sure
enough good trader, most likely he'll eyeball the item in question like he's never seen it before, take a chew, and tell you he
don't rightly know *what* the darn thing's worth and that he
ain't real sure he wants to get rid of it anyway. He'll go on to
tell you, though, that he did hear tell of an ol' boy who give
$X.00 for one almost identical. That same fella figgered he got
a real bargain 'cause he bought it from an ol' boy who was
married the first time to the current wife of a second cousin of
the buyer's second wife's uncle.

Don't get addled or flustrated with the kin line. Instead,
come back with one of these: "I come to the same conclusion
long ago about tradin' with kin that the ol' male skunk come to
about makin' love to the female skunk. After about ten minutes of that activity, he said he'd enjoyed about all of it he

could stand." —or— "Ain't it pitiful, though, the way kin will get into your money sock faster and deeper'n almost anybody?"

Let him chew on that along with his Union Standard tobacco for awhile, and talk about somethin' unrelated. Then, when you figger the time is ripe, ask: "Well, what'll you take for it?" —or— "What's your bottom dollar on the ol' thing?"

He'll come back with somethin' along the lines of: "I don't rightly know how to price it. What would you *give* for it?"

You say: "I never did like to price another man's goods. What do you reckon you have to *have* for it?"

He'll hem and haw for awhile, then ask you $X.00. No matter how good it seems, don't never agree to a first askin' price. Best is to snicker and snort some and say: "Man, you must think I rolled in on the last punkin wagon, or somethin'." —or— "My mama only raised one fool, and it wasn't me."

After you acted like you got over the shock of such a high price, make your counter offer, and make it way less than his first price. He *could* say now: "I sure do hate to let it go for that, but seein' as it's you and all, I guess you done bought it."

To be real honest, though, this kind of get-it-done-quick ain't real likely. More likely is that *he'll* playact shocked and use one of your own shock lines against you. Finally, though, if you stick to him like a fly to flypaper, you can darn sure get the item bought. There ain't never been a man borned who wouldn't sell what he's got if the money's right.

MOVIN' ON

If you got one of the fast-turn items listed out below, you can just pay the man and throw it in the back of your pickup to set on like a hen does her eggs—that is, 'til *you* run acrost some ol' boy thinks he needs it in *his* business. If it's a slow-turn item, better take it on to the house and leave it off in the yard for later.

Fast-Turn Items

Old bathtubs, sinks, commodes	Bedsprings
Railroad ties	Tires
Utility poles	Metal barrels
Beagle pups	

Slow-Turn Items

Pre-1947 tractor parts	Broke refrigerators
Bird cages	Broke air conditioners
Broke lawn mowers	

LAST TRADIN' NOTE

If instead of you buyin' the item in question with actual U.S. dollars, you can trade another item for it—like for instance, you offer to give an ol' cattle prod for a fairly new tractor tire—the ol' boy may ask you for some "boot." This ain't got nothin' to do with manly footwear. Boot is somethin' extry to make up the difference in value between your item and his. Could be money; could be most anything.

JOCKEYIN' HORSES

Tradin' on them ol' ponies ain't a bad way to make a livin', but it ain't an easy one neither. Some of the onryest, shrewdest ol' boys in the world handle ponies, and a man's got to be on his toes to keep ahead of 'em. In addition to the horse traders, of course, is the horses themselfs, who can be almost as unpredictable and cantankerous as the ol' boys who handle 'em.

Tryin' to buy a sure enough good pony worth the cap takes a lot of know-how. What you got to keep in mind is that you ain't buyin' it for yourself, but for someone who probably

don't know hush puppies from pork fries when it comes to horses. This means that the horse's *looks* is more important than his can-do ability.

The same technique we done give out for general tradin' works for horses, too. There are, however, some special things you got to know for tradin' on horses in particular, since fast-turn is real important. Unlike fence posts and motor parts, horses will eat into your profits with feed and care items if you hold on to 'em too long.

HORSE CENTS

- Never trust a fella who tells you he's got a horse that rides good but don't look so good. Last time we bought that story, we ended up with a pony who was blind in one eye and couldn't see too well out of the other.
- Check for bald spots that has been covered over with shoe polish.

- Never kick an ol' pony in the tail end with your spurs on to test his reflexes. We've seen several men drug the length of a pasture through all sorts of undesirable organic matter on the strength of gettin' their spurs caught in some ol' pony's matted tail. It ain't the best way to ride one.

SELLIN' POINT LINES TO USE

Speed:

"This horse is so fast he can run from daylight to dark in an hour."

"He's got a lot of run about him."

"This ol' pony can really gather up some of that yonder."

Gait:

"He's a real toe-tapper."

Good Breedin':

"He's bred higher than a peckerwood hole."

"He's bred in the purple."

Fancy Markin'—Stockin's, Socks, Blazes, Etc.:

"He's got more chrome than a Cadillac."

"He's lit up like a Christmas tree."

TAKIN' UP THE SLACK

If you can't make the rent and put food on the table by tradin' around, you'll need to take up the slack someways.

TRUCK FARM

Possible choices are:
- Have a wife who works out.
- Have a big garden and a wife who'll put things up by cannin' or freezin' 'em.
- Have a wife who works out.
- Have a big garden and a wife who'll sell the produce on the highway from the back of the pickup.
- Have a wife who works out.

HAVIN' SOME FUN: WHAT TO DO WHEN YOU AIN'T DOIN' NOTHIN' IS DRINKIN' AND DANCIN'

Since life's mostly work with a little time for fun, a man's got to make sure the little time is well spent. *Best* way to spend it is drinkin' and dancin'. Here's general directions on doin' both redneck style and doin' 'em good.

WHERE-TO: JOINTS, HONKY-TONKS, CLUBS AND BARS

"Let's go jukin'" is the battle cry of the ready-to-party redneck. What this means is let's hit a place where they got a jukebox and play it to beat the band. The kind of place you hit depends on the kind of time you got it on your mind to have, bein's as there's a wide range of possibilities.

Joints: Short name for beer joints, where you got your choice of drinkin' beer or drinkin' beer. They're mostly waterin'

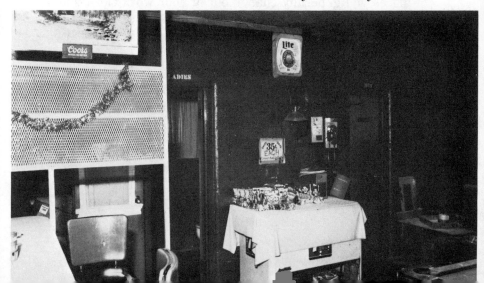

holes for the boys, with only an occasional female passin'
through. Music to play pool and fight by is the kind they got
on the box.

Honky-Tonks: Affectionately knowed as "tonks." These
places is a big step up in what you can get to drink, but not
much of a one in what they look like. Tonks usually serve
mixed drinks along with the beer and women along with the
men.

Clubs and Bars: These two is about the same thing. The kind
of places you generally change out of your work clothes and
into somethin' clean for. You'd also take a gal or a wife here
for a drink and a dance 'cause they generally got two
restrooms.

WHAT-TO: LONGNECK BUD, JACK BLACK, BLUE SOCK, CAT WHISKEY, AND HOMEMADE BEER

Everybody's got their own taste in beer, but if you're
serious about bein' a redneck you'll make sure yours is for
longneck Bud. Other beers'll get the job done, but a longneck
is the sign of a redneck without question. Reasons for this, if
you just *got* to know why you're doin' what we tell you, is:

- You can hold the bottle by the neck without coverin' up the label. Don't take no chatter to get a refuelin'.
- It's easier to hold a longneck when you're leanin' up against the bar or hunkered down somewheres.
- If you should happen to get crosswired with some ol' boy who's tougher'n a boot heel, a broke longneck bottle allows for a better deterrent to actual physical contact than a regular one.

TYPICAL DRINKS

Whiskey: Better order Jack Black or Blue Sock. These is the redneck names for Black Jack Daniels and Seagram's Crown Royal. Crown Royal is called Blue Sock on account of them little, blue drawstring pouches it comes in. Women like to use these for their curlers and makeup, but they generally don't like what a man's got to do to get 'em. They gotta empty the jug to give her the sack. Don't go takin' too many home or you could find yourself in a heap a hurt.

Homemade Whiskey: It's hard to beat Jack Black and Blue Sock, but there's one thing that'll do it: wildcat whiskey, also knowed as "cat," "white lightnin'," and "ol' loudmouth." The last name is the one that best describes the stuff, 'cause after only a few slugs of it a man's IQ can jump as much as fifty points and he won't be ashamed at all to say so. Most ol' boys who drink cat get nine feet tall and bulletproof in a hurry. Makin' your own whiskey ain't no big thing, but it is illegal. We'll tell you how if you want to give it a whirl, but we ain't advisin' you to.

MIXIN' AND WORKIN' OFF

In a barrel that'll hold 55 gallons, mix up:

1 lb. yeast
50 lbs. sugar
25 lbs. grain (corn or barley will work fine, but rye's
the best 'cause it's a soft grain and works off faster)

Top off the barrel with a layer of soft ground wheat, which makes what you call a "bran cap." It tells you when your whiskey's ready to cook off by turnin' upside down and sinkin' to the bottom of the barrel. The time for workin' off will vary considerable dependin' on the weather. In hot summertime it can take only two or three days; in cold wintertime it can take a lot longer.

When the bran cap sinks, what you got in your barrel is real strong beer—about thirty proof. Some folks stop here and bottle 'er up. But if you want cat, you got to cook it off in a still, which looks like this:

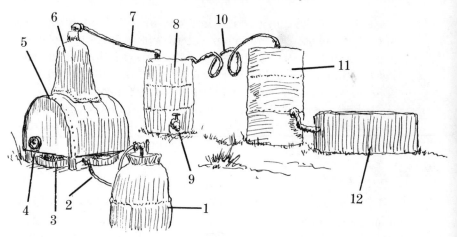

1. PROPANE GAS BOTTLE
2. GAS LINE
3. FIRE: TWO 55-GALLON BARREL LIDS WELDED TOGETHER WITH HOLES PUNCHED IN 'EM FOR A GAS RING
4. HOLE SO'S YOU CAN WASH OUT THE COOKER AFTER EVERY RUN.
5. COPPER COOKER
6. COPPER-LINED DOME
7. LEAD LINE
8. THUMP KEG TO CATCH ALL THE OL' FUSEL OIL AND IMPURITIES
9. OLD KITCHEN FAUCET FOR DRAININ' OFF THE REMAINS IN THE THUMP KEG
10. WORM, ALSO CALLED THE COOLIN' COIL. GOES DOWN THROUGH THE WATER IN THE COOLIN' BARREL.
11. COOLIN' BARREL
12. CUTTIN' VAT, ALSO CALLED THE CATCH VAT

COOKIN' OFF

Pour or pump the beer out of your mash barrel into the cooker through a strainer. Then all you got to do is keep a low fire under the cooker 'til the liquid is all cooked off. Don't let your fire get too hot or you'll puke your beer up into your worm (which means you'll send the liquid through the tubing). The idea is to keep just the steam flowin' through the tubes. The cold water in the coolin' barrel turns the steam back into the liquid that makes you feel single, see double, and pay triple if you drink enough of it.

The first drippin's that come out into the catch vat are about 190 proof. To get your cat to where it'll do you good rather'n do you in, let the *first* of the run stay in the vat and get cut down to size by the *rest* of the run, which gets weaker as it goes. It ought to even out at about 100 proof to be right.

When the run's finished, you got two choices. Either put it directly into your quart jars as is or put it into charred oak kegs to let it age a spell and smooth out a bit.

Hints and Facts

- To give your cat a nice amber-brown color, brown a little sugar or some peach-tree chips in the oven and put either in your batch. The sugar will dissolve, but you got to remove the chips after you got the right color. They don't go down easy.
- Don't worry about any small animals that find their untimely end in your mash barrel. The cookin' removes the impurities if you'll remove the remains.
- You can spot fellow cat drinkers by lookin' at the bridge of their nose. After a while, drinkin' from a Mason jar leaves a little depression where the rim rests.
- Old Maalox jars—and you'll have a-plenty around if you drink cat for long—make handy and safe travel-size containers.
- If you got to transport a big supply of cat somewheres, try this. Get yourself a enclosed horse trailer with a lace-up canvas curtain that hangs down inside the gate. Find an ol' horse with enough tail to spare and cut off a couple of feet of it. Tie what you cut off together at one end and stick it through the laced-up curtain so it looks like you're a-haulin' the horse rather'n the cat.
- Use the mash left in your barrel after you pour the liquid into the cooker for hog feed. They love it.

Homemade Beer: Homemade beer—either Choc beer or plain ol' home brew—is a lot stronger'n store-bought. It's alcohol content can get on up to the eighteen percent level, so you got to watch out it don't sneak up on you. You can cipher it out this-a-way:

Store-bought beer = 6%
Homemade beer = 18%
18% ÷ 6% = 3 times as dangerous to your health
  and social standin' = consume with caution.

Choc Beer

The name of this beer is short for "Choctaw," on account of that Indian tribe is supposed to be the original makers of it. We don't know as this is true and, to be real honest, we don't care much neither. It's good-tastin' and better-feelin', and that's what counts.

To make Choc, mix up in a cookin' pot:

15 gallons water
8 lbs. malt barley
½ of a ¼ lb. cake of hops

Put the pot over a low flame, uncovered, and let it stay there simmerin' pretty good for about six hours. When the time's up, pour the liquid through a strainer into another container. Let it cool and settle for about twenty minutes, then pour it back into the first container, which you've cleaned and rinsed out. Do this three times, waitin' twenty minutes each time.

After all three pourin's, wait for the temperature of the liquid to reach somewheres between 110 and 115 degrees, and stir in:

3 packages of dry yeast
All but 1½ cups of a 10 lb. bag of sugar

Now the completed mixture's got to work off. In a fairly warm room—about seventy-five or eighty degrees—this will take about twenty-four hours. While it's workin' off, the liquid will fizzle up, creatin' what's called a "boilin' cap." When your beer's worked off completely, this cap will settle to the bottom of your container. At this point you got what's called "green beer."

Pour the green beer into another container and let it settle again for twenty minutes. Do this four times if you want your beer to be real pretty and clear, makin' sure to wash out your containers each time you pour off. You gotta do this to get rid of all the settlin's. When you've done this all four times, add the 1½ cups of sugar you kept back out of the bag and stir it up real good. Let that sit for twenty minutes and you're ready to bottle.

Bottlin'

Beer is best bottled in them glass, quart-size soda pop bottles with the screw on lids. Wash 'em out good with soap and water and run 'em through the dishwasher without soap to sterilize 'em. Strain the beer through a woman's nylon stockin' as you pour it into the bottles. Screw on the lids, makin' sure to give 'em an extry turn with a pair of pliers for security's sake.

Agin'

Agin' your beer proper generally takes two weeks or so. If you want to hurry up the process a mite, put the bottles in your bathtub and draw enough hot water in it to reach up almost to the lids. When the water cools, drain it and repeat the process.

Hints and Facts

- Buy your wife a dishwasher and a year's supply of nylon stockin's. That's what you call smart shoppin'.
- If you use a #3 washtub for your cookin' pot, use it *only* for that. Don't never use the one you keep gasoline in for soakin' clean your truck parts or the one you use to feed the hogs from.
- Before you go to bottlin' be darn sure that the sugar has worked off completely. If it ain't, you'll soon enough know it 'cause them bottles'll go to poppin' their tops and blowin' their lids like nothin' you ever seen before. We know of an ol' boy who had to make arrangements with his neighbors for the use of their restroom facilities on account of he bottled his beer too soon. Only a honyock would step foot into a bathroom after hearin' one bottle of a batch of beer pop off.

Home Brew

There's a definite difference in taste between Choc beer and home brew even if there's not much a-one in the effects. Home brew's got what you might call a definite "whang" to its taste.

To make home brew, mix up:

1 5 lb. can of malt/hops syrup
15 gallons of boiled water

The rest is exactly the same as for makin' Choc, only you don't cook home brew. That's why you boil the water first.

EXTRY SPECIAL SECTION: OKLAHOMA LIQUOR LAWS

Redneck drinkin' is prob'ly so much fun 'cause it's so darn hard in most places rednecks live. Texas, for instance, works under a system of liquor laws called "county option." The option is whether a county ought to be "wet" or "dry." If it options for "wet," a man *can* buy a beer or whiskey when he's inside its boundaries. If it options for "dry," he *can't*. This kinely helps explain why Texans drive such big cars and why they drive around in 'em so much. A man's got to go where a man's got to go, and in that state he's often got to go a fur piece to get a jug.

Oklahoma, U.S. of A., though, is the state that skins the cat when it comes to drinkin'; the laws are so confusin' they drive a man to drink. In Oklahoma they sell two grades of beer: 3.2% and regular like everybody else in the country sells. Now, 3.2 is the only beer a man can fuel up on in the honky-tonks and joints, and that ain't enough to rev up even a scared jack rabbit to hoppin' speed. 3.2 is also the only beer a man can buy *cold* in any store. To drink a cold *real* beer, a man's got to plan ahead and make a trip to the liquor store enough in advance to cool it before downin' it. It's a hard life for those who weaken.

It's Oklahoma's complicated procedure for gettin' a mixed drink that's really enough to frazzle the best of folk, though.

This situation has resulted in what we call the "redneck brownbagger," 'cause in Oklahoma a man's got to take his *own* bottle into a bar and drink from that rather'n goin' into a place and orderin' up a ready-made drink.

THE SIGN OF A REDNECK
BROWN-BAGGER

It works this-a-way. The law says that places that provide mixed drinks got to consider themselfs "private clubs." None of these places got any windows and all of 'em got locked doors. To get in, a man's got to ring a doorbell and wait for the door to get opened from the inside. The person goin' in is supposed to have bought a membership card and have it with him so's he can show it to the person answerin' his ring. He's also supposed to be totin' his own bottle in a sack.

When he's let in, the man gives his bottle to the barmaid, she writes his name on it big as you please, and he orders his drink that's got to have the contents of his bottle as the mainest ingredient. The club don't keep *no* liquor in stock, only the glasses, ice, and mixin's. The glass, ice, and mix that goes with the sauce is called a "set-up," and that's what a man pays for when he gets his completed drink from the waitress.

This sounds real complicated 'cause it is, but we got to be honest and admit that lots and lots of folk don't follow these rules exactly to the letter. Most clubs ain't never bothered to print up the membership cards all their customers is supposedly carryin'. Most of 'em has also got a rather overwhelmin' supply of almost full bottles behind the bar that various Dewaynes and Orvals must of "forgot" to take home with 'em when they left. A man who don't "remember" to bring his own jug can kinely get mistook for Dewayne or Orval if he plays his cards right, and manage to get a drink. It ain't no hill for a climber.

HOW-TO: JUST FOLLOW IN MY BOOTSTEPS

From the make-your-heart-pound sound of the Cotton-Eye Joe to the make-your-heart-ache beauty of a real slow buckle polisher, dancin' is one of the best entertainments they are. While watchin' folks in tights and tutus don't do much for us rednecks, gettin' out on a sawdust-covered floor and participatin' in the activity of *real* dancin' darn sure does.

Dances You Got to Learn to Redneck Right

WITH A PARTNER

Two-Step	Cotton-Eye Joe
Western Swing	Schottishe
Western Waltz	Sweetheart Schottishe

Line Dances Where Everybody's Your Partner

Four Corners	Slappin' Leather
Kicker Hustle	Okie Stomp
Cowboy Hustle	The Skip
Texas Freeze	

Picture Directions for the Two-Step

SLIDE

SLIDE

SLIDE

LIFT

STEP/LIFT

Repeat 'til the songs done and/or you're plumb wore out.

STYLE POINTERS

- Hunker down a mite; bend your knees and lock 'em in place.
- Don't never lift your feet too far off the floor.
- Don't *never* bounce.
- Keep a serious look on your face.

TO-WHAT: ANOTHER SOMEBODY DONE SOMEBODY WRONG SONG

Now that you've got your ol' self fueled up and have learned how the steps go, we'll tune you in to the titles of the music you'll be a-movin' to.

The Redneck Hit Parade

"I Love My Redneck, My White Socks, and My Blue Ribbon Beer"
"She's Actin' Single, I'm Drinkin' Doubles"
"She's Got a Drinkin' Problem, and It's Me"
"Now I Lay Me Down to Cheat"
"D-I-V-O-R-C-E"
"I'm the Only Hell My Mama Ever Raised"
"I'm Gonna Love You Till the Cows Come Home"

"Don't Come Home a-Drinkin' with Lovin' on Your Mind"
"If Drinkin' Don't Kill Me, Her Memory Will"
"Let's Go Get Drunk and Be Somebody"
"She Belongs to Everyone But Me"
"Ask Any Old Cheater Who Knows"
"Bombed, Boozed, and Busted"
"Makin' Love Don't Always Make Love Grow"
"Your Body is an Outlaw"
"Married, But Not to Each Other"
"She Don't Have to Stop and Rock the Baby"
"Your Lovin' Couldn't Take the Walkin' Out of My Shoes"
"Love is a Two-Way Street (And She's Makin' a Lane Change)"
"You Just Loved the Leavin' Out of Me"
"It Don't Feel Like Sinnin' to Me"

Redneck Songs Still Waitin' to Be Wrote

"Meet Him in the Roundhouse, Effie; He Can't Corner Ya There"
"She Broke My Heart and I Broke Her Jaw"
"I Used to Kiss Her on the Lips, But It's All Over Now"
"Come Out of the Wheat Field, Granny, You're Goin' Agin the Grain"
"I Met Her at the River, But She Wouldn't Come Across"
"She Broke My Heart, But I Love Her Still"
"Get Off of the Cookstove, Granny, You're Too Old to Ride the Range"
"I Could Tell She Was a Coal Miner's Daughter by the Slack in Her Drawers"

EXTRY, EXTRY SPECIAL SECTION:
A NIGHT AT THE DEW DROP INN

Most every town that's got any number of rednecks livin' in it at all has got a Dew Drop Inn, even if it ain't called by that name. Goin' out to "drop a little dew," as the ladies is fond of callin' it, is as necessary to bein' a redneck as eatin' fried chicken for Sunday Dinner. In towns where there ain't, thank the Lord, a lot of nighttime entertainment (of a legal and organized sort, anyway), dancin' and meetin' up with your friends to down a few, swap a few lies (first liar ain't got a chance), and get a gander of the local high steppin' fillies tops the list. It sure beats sittin' around and watchin' the grass grow.

It's kinely tough to let you on to the excitement and flavor of the experience of spendin' a night at the Dew Drop, but we thought a little play-like might at least give you an inklin' of what you been missin' sittin' in opry halls (excluding the Grand Ole, of course) or watchin' the television set at home.

"Would you keer to daince, ma'am?" —or— "Would you like to come out and hold on to me whilst I dance to this song?"

Buckle Polisher—or—Belly Rubber

"Are you married?" "No, but my wife is."

"My name is Slats, as in bed. Last name is Simmons, as in Beauty Rest."

"Let's get out of here and go somewheres else. This place is *crawlin'* with ex-husbands." "How many you got out there?" "Four, at last totin'."

"I'm most beholdin', darlin'."

"Cut Out the Lights, the Party's Over"

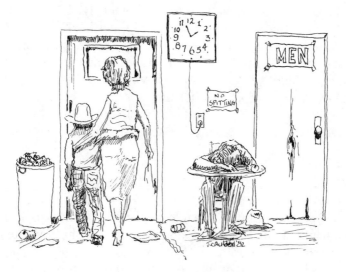

A MAN'S A MAN FOR ALL THAT

HUNTIN': THAT AIN'T BAMBI, THAT'S DINNER ON THE HOOF

Deer Huntin'

Them folks who like to think they're "nature lovers" but who ain't never been in the woods except for a day at a time inside a camper-trailer like to raise a ruckus about shootin' somethin' as *cute* as a deer. Now, we don't hold much truck with sport huntin', but huntin' for meat to put on the table's a different thing altogether.

Nothin' makes us hotter'n to come across a deer carcass left behind by some honyock who was only interested in havin' the head to hang on some den wall. We get even hotter

everytime we hear tell of some ol' boy chowin' down on steak
or lobster and goin' on between bites about how deer huntin'
is *cruel* and *heartless* slaughter of the innocents. Guess them
cows and lobsters ain't cute or innocent enough to bother
most folk.

If Walt Disney ever made a movie about how a lobster
baby lost his mama the way he done about Bambi, the folks up
north who make a livin' haulin' in them ol' grandsnappies
would be standin' in welfare lines. Obviously, Elsie the Cow
ain't never won no hearts in a big way, neither. Even though
her and her young 'uns been on TV and in magazines all
dressed up in people clothes and talkin' and singin' like real
people, nobody's tryin' to shut down the feedlots or boycott
McDonald's on account of her and hers.

Deer meat is some of the best eatin' meat they are. We'd
rather have venison than beef steak any day of the week.

Spotlightin' for Deer

Just like in everything, there's a right way and a wrong
way of deer huntin'. The right way involves huntin' during
season and havin' the license and the deer tag the government
tells a man he's got to have. Now, we ain't real fond of *nobody*
tellin' us how, when, or where to do *nothin'*, but if you include
deer huntin' in your becomin'-a-redneck effort, we advise you
to do like the government says. Leastways in the beginnin'
when you're new to it.

Spotlightin' for deer definitely *ain't* doin' like the government says. A man gettin' caught at it is goin' to lose his gun,
his truck, and his freedom for awhile, not to mention a sockful
of money in fines. Spotlightin' is deer huntin' at night with the
help of a high-powered spotlight that a man kinely shines
around the woods 'til it hits on the eye of an ol' deer and
freezes him up long enough for you to bag him.

Although we ain't tellin' you to, if you do hunt this-a-way,
you better be darn sure you can tell the difference between a
deer eye and a cow eye, cause they ain't all that easy to tell
apart by shape in the dark. Some ol' farmer who loses his cow

to a deer hunter might not be as reasonable about your doin's as the law is. Losin' your truck ain't real good, but bein' peppered with buckshot is a darn sight worse.

Little Game

This is as excitin' and good-meat producin' as huntin' deer. Course, you got to get more to have enough to feed every-body, but the gettin's half the fun.

SQUIRRELS

Either a gray or a fox squirrel makes for good eatin' whether it's fried, baked up in a meat pie, or boiled so's you can use the gravy for dumplin's. Best way to find a bushy tail is to find a hick'ry tree, 'cause they surely love hick'ry nuts. If you want to bring the squirrels to you rather than exertin' yourself lookin' for them, you can call 'em. All you got to do is to lick the back of your hand, pucker up like you was goin' to lay a smacker on some li'l darlin', and suck hard enough to make a kinely high squeak. Nine or ten of the little squeaks done real fast will get the local squirrels' attention right quick. Another good way is to save a paw from a squirrel you already bagged and rattle the toenails against the bark of a tree.

RABBITS

Early in the mornin' and late in the evenin' rabbits come out to feed themselfs. If you get your tail out and look for 'em, you can fix it so they'll feed you instead. Like most decent folk, rabbits don't never wander too far from home, so once you find their home you can usually fill up your skillet pretty easy. Look for rabbits in old buildin's, abandoned car bodies, fence-post piles, and old piles of junk of all sorts. If a man's a trader with a respectable inventory in the yard, he can usu-ally scare up enough rabbits right outside his own front or back door to feed the family.

Quail

There's only one thing prettier than listenin' to a bobwhite quail call out in the woods, and that's a-listenin' to him sizzle up in the skillet. Quail are real consistent in their habits, so once you find a covey you can walk 'em up time after time. Dawn and dusk are good times to go after quail, 'cause their usually a-movin' around these times. They come out to dust, peck at gravel, and water up. Never shoot a covey down to less than five or six birds. Since a covey is like a family, kinely bandin' together for protection and warmth, shootin' into one too heavy might well wipe out the clan completely.

TRAPPIN': WHY WOULD A MAN SHOOT A TRAP? THEY AIN'T GOOD EATIN' AND THEY'RE DEAD ANYWAYS.

While huntin's a skill, trappin's an art. The true trapper's got to be smarter'n the animals he's aimin' to trap, and that ain't always the case with a lot of folks. While trappin' don't always put meat directly on the table, sellin' the hides and furs can help a man take up the slack by addin' to his yearly income.

What to Trap and How to Trap 'Em

Polecat (Skunk)

Skunks like tainted bait best, so you got to keep rotten mice, eggs, or fish around to bait your traps with. If you're plannin' on usin' scent to attract the polecat rather'n bait, we got a good receipt for the best. Just mix up a half-dozen rotten eggs and the scent of one skunk real good.

Here's a couple of other things about skunks you might like to know. First, the oil of a skunk, if you render it real careful and don't burn it, is a good remedy for the croup. Second, given the fact about skunks that makes 'em most famous, you got to be aware of how to avoid or get rid of the scent from yourself if you want to keep your family and friends. To avoid gettin' it on your hands, grease or oil 'em good before handlin' the critter. To wash off what you wasn't smart or lucky enough to avoid, use benzine, gasoline, or cider vinegar. If you bury your clothes in damp ground overnight, it'll draw the smell clear out of 'em.

MINK

Talkin' about trappin' these critters always puts us in mind of the ol' boy whose wife asked him one day if he wouldn't please get her a mink. "Sure, sugar," he answered. "Bein' as I'm a man of means, I'll get you two. All you got to promise is that you'll keep the cages clean." The receipt for the scent that draws mink to a trap is this:

> Cut up a fish into small pieces and put 'em in a mason jar. Let this stand in a warm place, uncovered, until it's completely rotten and in a liquid form. Add the female parts of at least one female skunk you took durin' matin' season.

FOX

These little devils is smart, like their name suggests. Any scent of man around a fox trap and there ain't no way you're goin' to get one. There's two good scent receipts for foxes.

> Remove the fat from one or two skunks, chop it fine, and put it in a pickle bottle. Cut up two mice and add 'em to the fat. Let this rest two weeks 'til everything is completely decomposed. Then add the scent of two skunks and five or six muskrats. Keep the bottle covered so the flies won't blow it, but not too tight.

—or—

Let the meat of one muskrat rot in a jar, then add a few ounces of strained honey and half an ounce or so of musk.

Wolf or Coyote

Best to use the urine of the same that you've let stay in a bottle 'til it's rancid. You can also get by with a mixture like the followin':

Put ½ lb. raw beef in a jar and let it stay there two weeks or 'til the odor is as bad as it can be, whichever comes first. Then add 1 quart liquid prairie dog oil, ½ oz. assafoetida dissolved in alcohol, and 1 oz. pulverized beaver castor and mix it up good.

FISHIN': TROTLINES AND TELEPHONIN'

Looky now, we're sure some of you unschooled folk think that fishin' is only somethin' an ol' boy does with a pole. For them that's got time to fritter away and who have only a middlin' appetite for fish, we reckon this method of pullin 'em in one at a time will do. But most of us has got to spend our time makin' a livin' and insist on sittin' down to a man-size mess of catfish. So, we're goin' to tell you about two ways of gettin' the job done in a big way and fast: trotline fishin', also called "juggin'," and telephonin', also called "crankin'." The first is legal, long as you follow the rules and regulations. The second is flat out against the law. Game wardens tend to think of telephonin' as unsportin' like. If they catch you at it, you'll be a-hauled in instead of the fish.

Trotlines Ain't Got Nothin' to Do With Horses

The handy thing about trotlines is that once you put 'em out, they do all the waitin' around for a bite. You can go on about your rat-killin', rememberin' that the law tells you to run the lines once a day. Course, any man with a lick of sense don't need to be *told* to do this. If you don't pull in the catfish every day, you ain't goin' to have fresh cat.

The law also tells you how long you can make the line and how far apart you got to space your hook lines that hang down

from the main line. If you space your hook lines closer than the law allows, you are doin' what is called "snag linin'," 'cause fish swimmin' under your line got a better chance of gettin' snagged than of gettin' by. Some folks, none *we* know, of course, do this a-purpose. It saves 'em the time they would otherwise spend baitin' the hooks and the money they would of spent buyin' the bait, since trickin' the fish into bitin' at the hook ain't the idea here.

Trotlinin' is also called juggin' 'cause a man's got to fix a jug of some sort on each end of the line so's he can keep it floatin'. Also, this a-way, he'll have an easier time finding his own line when he comes out to get his fish. The basic idea is to tie each end of a long line to a jug. You leave a little extry line out past each jug so's you can tie a weight on each end that will kinely anchor your line where you put it. Or, you can tie one of the extry pieces to a tree on the bank and weight down the other. The most common jugs used is them plastic gallon milk jugs, old bleach bottles, and empty antifreeze containers.

Hangin' down from the main line is your hook lines. You bait each hook as you ease your boat along puttin' out the line. Minnows will do for bait, but they cost money and there's lots of free possibilities that'll work just as well. If you've killed and dressed your own hog for the deep freeze, use the liver. Or, if you been up and at it early enough to have bagged a few squirrels or rabbits for breakfast, use their innards.

Runnin' the lines is easy. All they are to it is to take yourself to one end of the line, cut the motor, and pull yourself along the line checkin' each hook as you go. Pull in the cat you caught, throw back the gar, weeds, and other noneatable catches, and rebait your hooks.

Telephonin': Reach Out and Catch Some Cat

We're only tellin' about this way of fishin' 'cause an ol' boy we won't name told us how: We want to get it clear right now that we wouldn't never engage in no activity this illegal. Whether you try telephonin' or not comes under the headin' of your business. We're really tellin' you how to do it so's you don't break the law accidentally out of ignorance.

The main ingredient in telephonin' is the mechanical insides of an old crank-style telephone. To make this into an electric fishin' pole, you attach a long line of insulated wire to each of the two poles you find in the works. You then strip a few inches of the insulation off of the end of each line and attach a metal weight on each. Old spark plugs or metal washers work just fine.

To actually use your telephone, you just take your boat out to a deserted spot on the lake and throw the two lines out from the boat in opposite directions. Then just give the crank a few good turns, sendin' out the resultin' electricity into the water. The man-made lightnin' you send off addles the cat-

MAIN INGREDIENT OF TELEPHONIN'

fish, and directly they'll come floatin' to the top of the water and belly up. All you got to do is scoop up all you can in your net and drop 'em in the live-wells of your ol' boat.

Don't worry none about any fish you can't get scooped up. They ain't dead, just a mite shocked. They'll come to shortly, figgerin', *we* figger, that you was just some crank caller.

PLAYIN' SMART:
BOOKS YOU GOT TO READ IN

Real rednecks, of course, ain't burdened down with a lot of time for book readin'. They're too busy makin' a livin' and doin' around in general to sit and do nothin'. But if a man or a woman does find a few extry minutes here and there, the books listed out below is worth lookin' into. Readin' them will learn you somethin', anyways.

FOR HIM:
LOUIS L'AMOUR DON'T WRITE ROMANCES

Louis' books is valuable on account of they can learn you a lot about the *spirit* that makes the real redneck. Even though the stories in 'em ain't true ones, they got a lot of truth in 'em.

Louis writes books about plain ol' common folk who built this great country of ours. The good guys is all rednecks at heart. They got pride and strength and courage, and they don't rely on no one else but themselfs to do for 'em. The bad guys is more like a lot of non-redneck folks today, bein' generally money-hungry and not very friendly.

The Best of L'Amour

Hanging Woman Creek	*Yondering*
High Lonesome	*The Lonely Men*
Kid Rodello	*Ride the Dark Trail*
The Strong Shall Live	

One of L'Amour's Stories: "Flint"

James T. Kettleman is a rich cattleman from back east who finds out he's got a cancer and that he's goin' to pass on soon. He leaves back east and goes out west to die on account of when he was a motherless child, a western man named Flint took him in and taught him right thinkin'. He also leaves 'cause his schemin' eastern wife, Lottie, and her no-good father are tryin' to have him killed so's she can get all his money.

Out west he meets a real woman, Nancy, who runs her own ranch almost single-handed, and he falls in love with her. In the end, after lots of excitin' fights and horse chase scenes, Kettleman finds out from an ol' doc out west that the ol' doc back east who said he had a cancer was all wet. Turns out he's got ulcers rather'n a cancer and that he ain't goin' to die after all.

He hurry-up outsmarts all of them tryin' to do him in and take his money, saves Nancy's ranch, dumps that little fizzle, Lottie, and hitches up with Nancy. There's more to it than that, of course, but that's the main idea of the story.

FOR HER:
LIFE STORIES OF COUNTRY WESTERN
WOMEN SINGIN' STARS

If men ain't got much time for readin', womenfolk got even less. Some books, though, demands to be read. These two true stories of real women facin' real life problems is both educational and inspirational. Even though they both done made it big in music, they've stayed common. They ain't let fame and fortune lead 'em to the mistake of goin' above their raisin'.

Stand by Your Man—*Tammy Wynette*

A *real* good book to buy for the wife. Tammy showed real love for George and a real womanly attitude in all she tried to do. Even though she finally couldn't stand to stand by him no longer, she done real good for a long time before she left him. You might ought to cut out the last few chapters of this one before you give it to your wife.

Coal Miner's Daughter—*Loretta Lynn*

Another good one to give to the wife. What Loretta tells about puttin' up with from Mooney will make whatever *you* done or ever will do pale to nothin' in your wife's eye. Loretta's *still* puttin' up with it, last we heard. Give your wife *all* this book. Take her to see the movie version, too.

THE PICTURE SHOWS:
MOVIES RATED "R" FOR REDNECK

Modern movies ain't much good, and that's a fact. It's a cryin' shame when a man can't take his family to the movies on account of it costs more'n he makes in a week and they'd see and hear things used to be seen and heard only in things that come in a plain brown wrapper or got talked about in a locker room.

If you got to give in and go to see a movie show, go to the drive-in where you can take your own popcorn, beer, and pop for the kids. Go to see only Walt Disney, Burt Reynolds, Charles Bronson, or Clint Eastwood.

The only decent movies anymore are them replayed on the television. No redneck worth his longneck Bud has missed any of these:

They Died With Their Boots On	*Hang 'em High*
Lonely Are the Brave	*Ride Lonesome*
Bite the Bullet	*Shane*
The Alamo	*Raiders of Sunset Pass*
Hit the Saddle	*Man Without a Star*

Also, any movie that's got John Wayne, Lash LaRue, Smiley Burnette, Gary Cooper, or Kirk Douglas in it's a must.

TELEVISION: DALLAS *IS TOO RICH FOR REDNECKS*

Although there's them says watchin' TV will rot the brain unless it's that fancy educational TV, we feel it's the other way around. If a man picks his shows careful for himself and his family, they can all learn a lot of important things by watchin'.

REDNECK T.V. GUIDE

New Shows to Watch

Hee-Haw	*Little House on the Prairie*
Dukes of Hazzard	*Lawrence Welk*
Western Outdoorsman	*Real People*

Old Shows to Watch

Beverly Hillbillies	*Gunsmoke*
Andy Griffith Show	*The Big Valley*
Green Acres	*Wanted: Dead or Alive*
Real McCoys	*Rawhide*
Bonanza	*The Waltons*

Never Watch No Matter How Desperate You Get

Nothin' on Public Television except animal shows
Tennis matches or soccer games
Talk shows

Always Watch No Matter How Busy You Are

Horse races
Rodeos
Country-and-Western-star singin' specials

PLACES TO VISIT

The true redneck seldom never wanders farther away from his home place than where he's got kin livin'. And if *they* ain't real close in blood, they better stay pretty close in distance if they want to be visited. Sometimes, though, a man's just forced to take the family somewheres special, even if it *is* more'n an hour's drive round-trip from his place. Listed out below are some of the few acceptable redneck vacation or visitin' places, divvied up by state.

TENNESSEE

Nashville in general, 'cause it is Music City, U.S.A. It's the home, of course, of the Grand Ole Opry, where the only real music comes from. There are lots of other things to see and do there, too, so you can get your money's worth from the trip.

- Opryland, U.S.A. An amusement park that's as much fun for grown-up people as for young 'uns.
- Country Music Hall of Fame
- Elvis-a-Rama. Has a eighty-five-foot long and ten-foot tall mural of Elvis's life that they use as a backdrop for a light and sound show that's amazin'. This tells the story of the King's life from his humble birth to his untimely end.
- Confederama. While they play "Dixie" and "The Battle Hymn of the Republic," 5,000 play soldiers with guns flashin' and cannons puffin' real smoke recreate the battles

of Chickamauga and Chattanooga of 1863. Blood-stirrin'.

- Tours of Nashville. Lots of these to see the outsides of the famous singers' houses, includin' Johnny Cash's and Kitty Wells'. There's also tours to Opryland, The Country Music Hall of Fame, and Music Row. Our very most favorite is the one to the Jack Daniels Distillery.

- Not too far from Nashville, in Pigeon Forge, you can visit Silver Dollar City. This place is a identical replica of an old-timey mountain town. They got mountain music and lots of folk dressed up in ol' costumes doin' ol' things that we ought to still be doin'. For instance, makin' soap and candles and some other things folks buy now at supermarkets.

OKLAHOMA

- Oklahoma National Stockyards in Oklahoma City. Biggest cattle and hog auctions you ever did see.

- The Cowboy Hall of Fame, also in Oklahoma City. They got all kinds of western paintings that ain't just blobs of paint throwed on a board. They show real people doin' real things. The best part of the whole shootin' match is the Chapel of the Hats. In it, they got hats worn by all the famous folks you can think of. Under each hat is a little red light. Outside the chapel, where the visitors stand, is a board with names and buttons on it. When you punch the name of the man's hat you want to see, the little light goes on under it. It's real inspirational. But not too long ago somebody actually stole John Wayne's hat out of the place. That empty peg is a real depressin' sight.

- Will Rogers Museum, in Claremore. This is a real movin' tribute to one of America's greatest men, the one who said he never met a redneck he didn't like. Most interestin' thing of all is that they managed to fetch back the clothes Will and Wiley Post was wearin' when their plane crashed and they was killed. They got 'em in a glass display case inside.

- Robert S. Kerr Museum in Poteau. Biggest collection of barbed-wire samples to be found.

TEXAS

Almost anywheres will do here. But two must sees are:
- The LBJ Ranch outside of Austin.
- The Alamo in San Antonio.

BIG EVENTS YOU GOT TO MAKE

These once-a-year events is ones worth plannin' any vacation around. We got them broke down into states and months. To get the details, write the Chamber of Commerce of the town.

Tennessee

April .... Old Time Fiddlers Championships, Clarksville
Mule Day, Columbia
August .... Memphis Music Festival: A Tribute to Elvis, Memphis

Arkansas

October .... Tall Tales Contest, Eureka Springs
Turkey Tracks Bluegrass Festival, Waldron
November ...... World Championship Duck Calling Contest and Queen Mallard Pageant, Stuttgart

Texas

March .... Farm Show and Tractor Pull, Fort Worth
April .... Prairie Dog Chili Cook-Off and Pickled Quail Egg Eating World Championship, Grand Prairie
June .... Watermelon Thump, Luling
July .... Black-Eyed Pea Jamboree, Athens
August .... Armadillo Alympics, New Braunfels
Great Texas Mosquito Festival with Miss Quito and Mr. Quito Legs Contests, Cluce

Oklahoma

April .... Rattlesnake Hunt, Waynoka
May .... Rooster Day Celebration, Broken Arrow
July .... State Horseshoe Pitching Contest, Blackwell
Brick and Rolling Pen Event, Stroud
August .... Draft Horse and Mule Plowing Contest, Mangum
Watermelon Festival, Rush Springs
Sucker Day, Wetumka
September ..... Prison Rodeo, McAlester

RULES OF COW CHIP THROW

1. Two chips to each contestant. Chip thrown the farthest shall be the only one counted. If the chip breaks up in the throw, then the piece going the farthest will be counted.

2. Contestants in the men's and women's divisions must be at least sixteen years old.

3. Chips shall be at least 6 inches in diameter.

4. Contestants must select their chips from the wagon load provided by the B.S. Enterprises Committee. To alter or shape in any way, chips selected from the wagon, (except in rare instances a loose fragment may be removed, provided the removal does not render the chip less than (6) six inches in diameter) subjects the contestant to a (25) twenty-five foot penalty. Decision of the Chip Judge is final.

5. Contestants will be registered and numbered at the official registration desk and must be ready when their number is called.

6. The politicians and VIP class will be held prior to the World Champion events, and entrants will be entered only by contest officials.

7. Any sanctioned cow chip throwing contest held anywhere in the world must use the adopted international arena layout and measurements to qualify any record throw to be recognized officially in the book of recognized World's Records.

A sketch and layout with Official Measurements shown below:

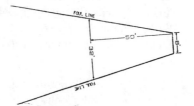

WORLD CHAMPION COW CHIP THROWERS

1981

MEN	Thane Wright	Levelland, TX	137'5"
WOMEN	Kay Hankins	Prairie Du Sac, WI	91'5"
VIP			
MEN	Bill Walten	Sanderson, TX	143'4"
WOMEN	Pam Ingram	Borger, TX	92'9"

ENTRY BLANK

WORLD CHAMPIONSHIP COW CHIP THROWING CONTEST
Beaver, Oklahoma—April 23, 1983 • $10.00 Entry Fee.

Please Bring This Entry Form with You—Do Not Mail.

Name_____Class ☐Men's Division
☐Women's Div.
Address_____·_____☐V.I.P.

City_____ State_____ Zip_____

Sponsoring Organization_____ Winner of Regional Contest?   ☐Yes   ☐No

EXTRY SPECIAL EVENT:
COW CHIP THROW

Every April in Beaver, Oklahoma there's a event that us rednecks like to call our own: The Annual Cow Chip Throwin' Contest. Cow chips is that animal's waste product and since we spend a lot of our time dishin' this out in a variety of forms, we got a special place in our heart for this spring fling. We're includin' an entry blank for the contest so's you can enter as soon as you think you're big enough to.

COW CHIP AWARD AND GENUINE COW CHIP

THE ANYTIME, ANYPLACE EVENT:
"LET'S RODEO"

Rodeo *is* America's number-one sport 'cause it was the first one we invented. Most of the events developed from the work done by the actual workin' cowboy that tamed the land we're a-livin' in so wild-like today. You ought not ever to miss one if you can help it. Real rednecks *never* do, whether it's on the TV, at the local Round-Up Club Arena, or even out of town. The biggest rodeo of 'em all is the National Finals held every year in Oklahoma City, Oklahoma.

Events

Bareback Ridin' This is a rough stock event. The cowboy rides a buckin' horse without the help of a saddle, reins, or stirrups. The horse has got what's called a "flank strap" on, which don't hurt him none but works to make him buck harder. The cowboy can only hold on to the riggin' with one hand, and he can't touch *nothin'* with the other.

Calf Ropin' In this event, the cowboy's got to rope a runnin' calf, stop his horse and dismount, run down the rope that's held taut by the horse, throw the calf, and tie together any three of his legs. He then throws his hands up high in the air to signal he's done. The tied legs got to stay tied for six seconds after the cowboy remounts his horse and slacks up on the ropin' rope.

Saddle Bronc Just like bareback bronc ridin', but with a saddle. The cowboy makes a qualified ride if he stays on for eight seconds and don't change hands, lose a stirrup, or touch himself or the horse with his free hand.

Bull Doggin' or Steer Wrestlin' With the help of a "hazer," who keeps the animal runnin' in a straight line, the cowboy's got to catch up to a fast runnin' steer, leap off of his horse, catch the steer by the head or horns, and throw him down on the ground. The steer's got to be down flat with his head and feet pointin' in the same direction for the cowboy to qualify. If the steer gets loose, the wrestler's got one step to get him again.

Team Ropin' or Headin' and Heelin' Two cowboys work as a team in this event. The first, the header, has got to rope the steer by the head, neck, or horns and dally his rope around the saddle horn. Then the second, the heeler, has got to lasso *both* hind legs and dally his rope.

Barrel Racin' For the most part, the only event for the cowgirl. This is a timed event where the cowgirl rides a cloverleaf pattern around three barrels in the arena. Fastest time wins.

Bull Ridin' This is the most dangerous and excitin' of all events, mostly on account of the fact that the Brahma bull weighs around 2,000 pounds and is mean as he can be. Also, the rank bulls they use for rodeo stock is *bred* for meanness. The cowboy rides the bull, holdin' on with one hand. To make the bull buck higher and faster and harder, there's generally a bell tied on him to kinely get on his nerves.

The Grand Entry March and the crownin' of the Rodeo Queen are two more excitin' parts of the rodeo.

Rodeo Terms and Phrases You Ought to Know and Toss Around

"Swallowed his head" . . . means the horse dropped his head real low and took to buckin' like blazes.

"Stalled on me" . . . means the buckin' horse stopped buckin' and just stood there like an idiot.

"Drawed a good 'un" . . . means the cowboy got the number of a *real* bad one to ride.

"Rank" . . . means the animal is *real* mean and nasty.

"Heck of a wreck" . . . what the bucked or throwed cowboy has had.

"Break the barrier" . . . means to leave the chute and head out into the arena too soon. Used in calf ropin', team ropin', and steer wrestlin'.

"Dally" . . . means wrappin' the ropin' rope around the saddle horn two times.

"Double hocker" . . . means a clean catch of both hind feet for the heeler in team ropin'.

"Markin' the horse out" . . . means the cowboy is getting good spurrin' action, rakin' the horse from the break in its shoulders back toward its flank.

"Piggen String" . . . what the calf roper uses to tie the calf's feet together after he's roped and throwed him.

"Hooey" . . . the half-hitch knot the cowboy makes with the piggen string.

8

Usin' Your Head for Somethin' Other'n a Hat Rack: Thinkin' Redneck Style

YOU'LL PROB'LY NOTICE right off that this here chapter on thinkin' is measurably shorter'n most a the others in the book. Don't be a-goin' and a-gettin' the idea this means rednecks don't think much. T'ain't so. We darn sure do. But we reckon it ain't no real use to fret and stew over things you can't do nothing much about, so we keep it down as much as possible. We realize, though, that a man's no man without opinions. While everybody ought to come up with their own, some things is so obvious there ain't no shame in a man's own ideas on 'em bein' real close to them of other men he respects. If you let on that what's given out below is what you think about these frequently jawed on subjects, you'll be close to dead center of redneck thinkin'.

RELIGION

Everybody ought to have some.

GUNS

Everybody ought to own some.

BIG BIDNESS

We all know big bidness is out to take over this here country. No matter who says what about this subject, you ought to shake your head real slow from side to side and say, "If you think it's bad now, just wait 'til they done took over farmin'. We can learn to live with two-dollar-a-gallon gas, but when we're a-payin' five dollars a loaf for bread or facin' a trumped-up 'wheat shortage,' we're all a-goin' to feel it, pard."

BIG GOV'MINT

The gov'mint ain't got no bidness a-messin' in other folks' bidness, be it private bidness or bidness bidness. All a them give-away programs has done had the result a makin' countless men and women lazy and thiefs for the most part. The Democrats want to give it all away to them that don't *want* to work for it in the form of welfare, food stamps, and the rest. The Republicans want to give it all away to them that don't *have* to work for it in the form of tax breaks and the like. Gov'mint ought not go no higher than the county level, so's a man could at least get to know the ones stealin' him blind. Gov'mint ought to tend to roads and such and leave a man alone.

THEM: YANKEES AND OTHER FOREIGNERS

While we hate it in the worst way to be inhospitable, the ol' "y'all come" idea's been took too far, now. It's a cryin' shame to take America away from the real Americans. We

got to be fair, though, and say that the internal foreigners in
this country ain't much better'n the external ones. Yankees
on the east side and hippies on the west make us feel kinely
surrounded by the former. They talk funny and got ideas
crazy as can be imagined. It wouldn't be so bad if they just
stayed where they belonged, but they all got the bee in their
bonnet that all of a sudden *our* part of the country is a nice
place to settle in, on account of its wide open spaces and all.
They ought to have sense enough to realize that if they keep
a-herdin' in at the rate they're a-goin', our spaces won't be
neither wide or open for long. We ain't too pleased with the
big exportin' of our wheat and oil out to anywhere foreign, in
or out of the United States, but sendin' out's preferable over
havin' 'em come here to use it up.

EDUCATION

While formal education ain't nothin' to be sneered at exactly, this country's in the mess it is today partly on account
of the over-educated idiots we got a-runnin' it now and have
had a-runnin' it for quite a spell. Book learnin' cut with a little
common sense is fine, but most a them who got higher edu-
cated must tie up their horse sense at the college hitchin' post
and leave it there permanent. What we know for a fact is that
while education is good for polishin' off the rough spots and
makin' a man good at talkin' to others just like him, it don't
make a damn when it comes to makin' money, makin' friends,
or just plain makin' a man.

KIN

The single most important thing in life. This great country
of ours was built on the idea of the family; helpin' each other
out when times is bad and sharin' the happiness when times is
good. A man owes his first allegiance to his mama and daddy
and any brothers and sisters he's got, then to all that's con-

nected to him by blood and marriage out in all directions far as it goes. If people would stay put and not be a-pullin' up their roots and a-movin' around so much, we'd all be a darn sight better off than we are now.

LIFE IN GENERAL

Life is kinely like dancin' with a fat woman—you never know which way she's a-goin' to go, and there ain't a darn thing you can do about it anyways.

9

Little Things Mean a Lot: Points of Style Redneck Style

ALL THEM LITTLE FINISHIN' TOUCHES THAT KINELY PULLS THINGS TOGETHER

ONCE YOU GOT all the major changes we been a-jawin' about kinely drawed in, you can go to workin' on refinin' the crude product. The little details in this here chapter are what amounts to the subtleties of redneckin', the little stylish touches that say out loud and clear the kind of man a man is. All these little things finish you off like the cream gravy does the biscuit or the top stitchin' does the shirt.

DIPPIN' AND CHEWIN' AND ROLLIN' YOUR OWN

Although there sure ain't nothin' *not* redneck 'bout a cigarette, especially if it's a roll-your-own from ol' Prince Albert hisself, there's nothin' quite like smokeless tobacco to give out the idea that you're a redneck. It don't make no never mind, neither, whether you're chewin' tobacco or dippin' snuff. Havin' either a quid, which is your wad of tobacco, in your cheek or a dip, which is your pinch of snuff, in your lip will help you in several ways in your strivin' to become a redneck.

First off, the bulge itself, no matter which facial locale it's a-residin' in, will just plain and simple make you *look* more redneck. And, what with the unavoidable effect such a bulge has on your speechin', it'll darn sure make you *sound* more

SKOAL RING

redneck, too. Last off, all the little go-alongs—from the Skoal ring (the white, worn circle you get on your rear pocket from carryin' your can of snuff there) to the slight yellowin' of your lower lip and chin area—is real tellin'.

How to Chew

To begin with, you got to make the important choice of whether you're a-goin' to go with shredded tobacco in the pouch or a plug or a twist that comes in a solid chunk wrapped in cellophane paper. We feel kinely obligated to tell you that a beginnin' chewer is wiser to begin with the first, 'cause the ol' plug tobacco, especially Cotton Bowl Twist, is stouter'n cold chili and garlic. It'll darn sure knock the fire from your guitar, now.

If you decide, goin' against our well-meant warnin', to jump right in and begin with a plug, just roll back the paper a inch or so, take your ol' knife out of your pocket, and whittle off a chunk.

SHREDDED TOBACCO

If you're man enough to admit your own greenhand standin', grab up a pouch of shredded tobacco, reach in with your thumb and first two fingers, and pull out enough to make a good-size wad. Dependin' on the size of your jowls and how stout you think you are, this could be anywheres from the size of a new baby's fist to a saddle horn. Make sure to give what you got a little shake before you get your hand out of the pouch so's you knock loose any extry clingers. To avoid havin' all the shreds stuck all over your mouth like coconut on top of a cake, put the bunch in the palm of your cupped left hand and use the thumb of your right hand to mash it up into a ball that sticks together. If you're a southpaw, reverse the hands in this process. Make sure, too, that before you go to mashin' you pick out any stray stems. They don't rest too comfortable in a man's cheek.

When you got 'er balled up pretty good, tuck your quid into your cheek and waller it around a bit with your tongue to get 'er settled in to stay for a while. Whether you chew on the right or the left is the same kind of question as whether you put on your right pants' leg first or your left. It's sure a personal one and the answer is best left to you.

How long to hold on to an ol' chew's also a personal question. In general, though, if you're a nervous-type, a good-size quid'll last only 'bout an hour or two. If you're a calmer sort a man, the same size quid will most likely last half a day or 'til it's time to eat, whichever happens to come first. If your chaw ain't completely chewed out come eatin' time, just wrap it up in your bandana or in a paper napkin so it won't dry out, put 'er where she's handy, and pop 'er in again when you're done eatin'.

What to Chew

POUCH

Beech Nut Regular	Gold Star
Work Horse	Big Duke (A Man's Choice)
Chattanooga Chew (Easygoin'	Red Man (America's Best
Flavor Born in the South)	Chew)
Union Station	Levi Garrett
Red Horse	(The Granddaddy of 'Em All)

Plug or Twist

Taylor's Pride	Bull of the Woods
Red Man	Brown Mule
Cannon Ball	Day's Work (Taste
Cotton Bowl Twist	the Freshness)

How to Dip

Pry off the lid of the tin real easy-like so's you don't spill none. It's too darn high and too darn good to waste. Reach in with your thumb and first finger, take a pinch, shake off the extry, and tuck what you got left down between your gum and lower lip kinely off to one side or the other. Some folks take their snuff between their cheek and gum like it was chewin' tobacco, but we recommend that the right place is 'twixt the gum and the lip. Once you got your pinch settled in, don't worry about it none; it'll take care of itself.

What to Dip

BRAND

Copenhagen	Gold River
Happy Days	W.E. Garrett
Skoal	Hawken
Silver Creek	Honest Scotch

Note: There's also bubble gum chewin' tobacco and snuff for the li'l redneck.

How to Spit

Power and control, developed with a lot of practice, is the key to success here. You got to learn to project if you want to avoid them unsightly dribbles down your ol' chin. If it helps you any at all, imagine you're a-spittin' out a watermelon seed. While not identical, the two actions is similar.

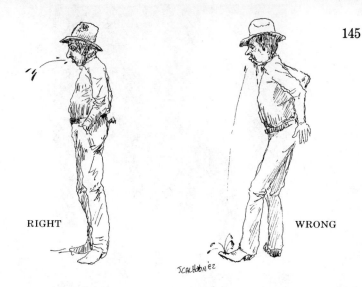

RIGHT

WRONG

What to Spit In

You got a wide range of possibilities here, from the most common and inexpensive to the high-dollar type receptacles. 'Bout the only thing you ought not spit into is, as the sayin' goes, the wind.

FOR COMMON FOLK

- A empty pop cup or one a them styrofoam coffee cups. Only real disadvantage to these is that they kinely lean toward tumpin' over pretty easy. A spit can tumpin' over onto somebody don't do a lot to win you their affection.
- Empty coffee cans. Good 'cause they hold so much more'n the first two mentioned possibilities, makin' it unnecessary to empty your can out so frequent. These are also a trifle more stable, lessenin' the possibility of it tumpin' over.
  Hint: If you're a considerate man when it comes to other folks nerves, you'll take the trouble to wad up a few paper towels or napkins in the bottom of the can. This'll take the edge off the beginnin' "pingin'" sound of the spit hittin' the empty can and also cut down the volume of the later-on "ploppin'" sound as the spit level rises. As an extry advantage, the paper'll absorb some of the spit and lessen the mess if the can should happen to get tumped over.

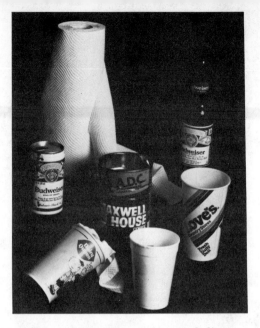

- Empty beer cans. For more advanced dippers and chewers only. Takes a skillful pair of lips to hit that little ol' slot.
- Empty beer bottle. Also only for the advanced spitter. The hole in the top of the bottle ain't much bigger than the slot in the top of the can. Words of Warnin': Never spit into a brown bottle, only a clear one. Unknowin' folks has been known to take a swig out of a spit-filled brown beer bottle. While this radically reduces a man's headache the mornin' after, it don't do much for his stomach at the time. If the drinker's an ol' boy big enough to go bear huntin' with a switch, the spitter's likely to take both a headache and a stomachache right fast. Since tobacco spit's quite a bit darker'n most beer, the clear bottles don't usually lead to anybody gettin' het up.

FOR HIGH ROLLERS

This group of spitteroos includes all a them containers made for the very purpose of spittin' into. These range from the many sizes of brass spittoons (from two to twelve inches high) made for stayin' at the house to the several kinds of travelers. The two most popular travelers are the "Kuspa-Kup," that's got an inverted funnel top for hidin' the spit from the eyes of the over-squeamish; and the "Li'l Cus," which has a weighted bottom so's it'll ride safely on the dash of the pickup.

If you got a wife that is kinely narrow-minded, you might ought to stick with the spittoons that you can toss out with the spit. Cleanin' out the permanent ones ain't a chore most women relish much.

When to Spit

Anytime you got to, within the confines of basic etiquette, of course. Keep in mind that there ain't no sense chewin' in your own juice. A man could get drowned that-a-way.

Where to Spit

Anyplace within reason. If you're a-travelin', out the window of the pickup is fine, but it does have its drawbacks. Window spittin' tends to result in long, brown streaks down the side of your pickup 'less you had the foresight to buy a brown one 'specially on account of this. It also ain't much appreciated by the young 'uns if they happen to be a-ridin' in the bed. Hounds don't seem to mind it much. There's many a man who orders his pickup without carpet so's he can let loose on the floor 'tween his legs as he's a-goin' and a-blowin'. Stoppin' at a gas station ever now and then to hose out your ol' truck ain't no big deal.

Inside of places you just got to kinely go with the flow, feelin' out the possibilities 'fore you settle in for a long stay. If you're at a joint like the local Dew Drop Inn, though, you might not ought to spit on the dance floor 'less there's sawdust on it. Folks might take to a-slippin' and a-slidin' more'n is seemly, even doin' the two step.

Rollin' Your Own

Homemade smokes, just like homemade anything, is far superior to ready-made. Gettin' good at rollin' your own takes as much practice as gettin' good at spittin' tobacco, but once you got it down pat you can count on this activity to signal you as a redneck. Prince Albert in the can is the number-one tobacco choice of rednecks. Bull Durham and Bugler run a close second to ol' P.A.

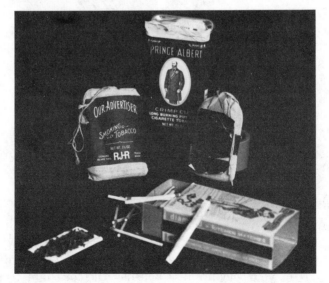

WALKIN' AROUND AND
JUST STANDIN' STILL

Men First

When you're a-walkin', keep yourself kinely rigid from the waist down and lope along in long strides without gettin' in any all-fired hurry. Let your arms swing kinely free and easy at your sides. Don't never walk with your hands in your pockets. It takes more time to get a handshake a-goin' or to tip your hat, and, besides that, it just don't look proper.

When you're a-standin' still, lean up back against a wall and put one leg up behind you for support. If you ain't around a wall, put your hands in your pockets, keep one leg straight down and stiff with all your weight on it, and put the other one out to the side with the knee a mite crooked. Never stand with your feet together.

If you get wore out a-standin', hunker down and sit on your heels with your forearms restin' on your thighs and your hands kinely danglin' 'tween your legs. Never put your hands down on the ground to steady yourself. If you ain't much on balance, practice this to home first 'til you get the hang of it. If you take a chair, sit in it backwards. If you take your hat off while standin', hunkerin', or sittin', hold it down in front of you kinely still-like. Never fan yourself with it no matter if it's hot as all blazes where you are. Fannin's for the womenfolk.

Then Women

When you're a-walkin', you ought to be everything but rigid from the waist down. If you're around any kind of a man at all, you won't need much advice on how to stand proper, 'cause you won't be a-standin' for long. When you're sittin', sit ladylike.

MAKIN' DO

Learnin' to make do is a high-level finishin' touch in learnin' to redneck proper. Makin' do's got two sides to it. The first is makin' use of what's on hand. *Never* buy somethin' special-made for a particular purpose. Most often it's a pure-D waste of money to do it that-a-way. If a man or a woman's got any sense about 'em at all, they can sure figger out a way of makin' somethin' make do for somethin' else. The second side involves avoidin' wastin' any part of anything. You got to train yourself to use all *of* everything you can *for* everything you can.

Below is some examples of what American know-how and enterprise can do on both sides of the makin' do issue. We've divvied up our for instances into them for women and them for men for easy reference.

Women

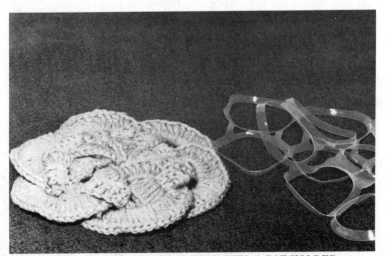

POP-CAN PLASTIC RINGS CROCHETED INTO A POT HOLDER

WHIPPED TOPPIN' TUB CROCHETED INTO
A CLOTHES PIN HOLDER

CROWN ROYAL BLUE
SOCK USED FOR
CURLER BAG

CLOROX BOTTLE CROCHETED INTO A SUN BONNET

HORSESHOE NAILS MADE INTO ART

HORSESHOE PLANT STAND

SNUFF GLASS AND MASON JAR FOR DRINKIN' GLASSES

Men

WHEELBARROW AND BEDSPRINGS USED AS PART OF FENCE

BEDSPRINGS USED AS GATES

MILK-CAN MAILBOX STAND

PUMP MAILBOX STAND

PLOW MAILBOX STAND

TOILET USED FOR PLANTER

STEEL DRUM USED FOR B-B-Q

BATHTUB WATERING TROUGH

A SPECIAL COMMENT ON BALIN' WIRE

Balin' wire is the king of make-do materials. This stuff, once you take it from the hay bales while you're feedin', is good for fixin' up just about anything from fences to the wife's washin' machine. Make sure you always got a-plenty layin' around the yard and in the back of your pickup so's you'll always have it handy. Tell any of them who complain about gettin' tangled up in it that poor folks got poor ways. That'll hush 'em up quick.

CURES

As a important subsection of makin' do, we're includin' what information we got about home cures. Though we've always been hard put to decide whether insurance salesmen, lawyers, or doctors is the sorriest lot, doctors prob'ly top the list. 'Stead of spendin' good money to be told you got what you already know you got and there ain't much that medical science can do for it, you're better off to take matters in your own hands. The ones we're a-givin' out here ain't nowheres near as costly as those you'll get from a doctor, and they're a darn sight more likely to take hold, too.

We're providin' only a few instances, but don't be fooled. There's a-plenty more out there for the askin'. Your best source of information in this area is your mama or your grandmama.

- Warts: Rub 'em with an ol' chicken bone, then throw the bone over your left shoulder and never look back on it.

  Tie a string around wherever it is for three days, then bury the string.

  Rub it with a used dishrag, then bury the rag.

- Freckles: Rub 'em with a used, wet diaper. You got to suffer to be beautiful, as my grandmama always said.
- Arthritis: There's them that swear by a few sprays of WD-40 lubricatin' oil rubbed into the sore joints.
- Whoopin' Cough: A glass of mare's milk will knock this out in a New York minute.

- The Itch/Bein' Bound Up/Stiff Joints: The water from boiled poke salad root.
- Just About Anything That Ails You: Sassafras tea. This is particularly good to drink in the spring on account of it thins your blood down and makes you better able to handle the heat of the summer.

STAYIN' COMMON

'Bout the highest compliment one man can pay another one in our part of the country is to say he's common. But stayin' common ain't as easy as it used to be and gettin' common for the first time is even tougher.

The most basic thought to keep in mind while a-workin' on this one is that bein' poor ain't nothin' to be ashamed of and bein' rich ain't nothin' to be proud of neither. No matter which you are, you might ought to follow the followin' pretty close if you're serious about makin' your ol' self over into a redneck.

- Stop and pass the time with everybody you meet no matter how much of a hurry you're in. Don't *never* meet a stranger.
- Ask about as many of anybody's family as you can call by name, then start in by relation. Don't forget the distant cousins, the in-laws, or the ex-husbands and wives.
- Don't never be windy 'bout what you got or how much money you're a-makin'. When folks ask how you're gettin' along, answer, "Kinely like the ol' sharecropper. I never had less and enjoyed it more." Say this even if you've just leased your mineral rights to 100 acres for $800.00 an acre.
- Keep a-callin' your mama and daddy "mama" and "daddy" no matter how old you get to be.
- Never wipe the top of a jug when a man offers you a taste out a his'n. Alcohol kills germs anyways.
- Don't be a-travelin' too far from home and a-gettin' no big ideas. If you do travel around some, pull a travel trailer, stop at kinfolks, avoid big cities, and don't stay gone too long.
- Borrow rather'n buy when you can, even if you can easy afford to buy. It's the principle of the thing. Loan when you got to.

HUMOR IN REDNECK FORM

Trainin' yourself to remember and to tell jokes that'll fit any situation, and honin' up your skill in tellin' 'em right, is an important style point in redneckin'. Jokes and stories pass the time, make people laugh, and oftentimes even go so far as to clear up things that's confusin'. When you're a-tryin' hard as you know how to explain how somethin' is or how somebody feels about the somethin' that is and you're not havin' much luck, you can most times help yourself along by means of a story or joke that pictures it out. You can lead into your joke with one of three lines: "It kinely puts me in mind of that ol' boy who . . .", "It's about along the same lines as that ol' gal who . . .", or "That's kinely like the . . ." Which one you choose depends, of course, on the joke.

What we're a-givin' you here ain't nothin' more'n a starter kit for a man's stock of jokes. To build up your inventory, all you got to do is to pay attention and take to storin' 'em up like a squirrel does acorns for wintertime. No matter how big your store gets, don't never hesitate to repeat your jokes time and time and time again. The wisdom of humor don't never grow old. Besides, a smart man'll more'n likely go to laughin' at your joke no matter how many times he's heard it before, 'cause he'll expect you to do unto him like he's a-doin' unto you.

A SAMPLER OF REDNECK JOKES

Grandma and Grandpa Huggins was a-sittin' on the front porch one day, a-rockin' and a-spittin' and a-watchin' their ol' rooster hit hen after hen all 'crost the yard. Grandma turned to Grandpa and asked, "Pa, why can't you do that?" Grandpa rocked forwards, spit into his ol' spit can, and answered, "Believe I could, Ma, if'n I had a different hen ever time."

Once there was this ol' boy who'd just took him a bride. Matter of fact, they was on the way home from gettin' hitched when all this took place. They was a-goin' along just fine, when the horse all of a sudden stumbled and broke her pace, kinely jarrin' the lovin' couple. The new husband stopped the wagon, got down, and walked up to the horse. "That's once," he said quiet-like. He got back in the wagon and they moved along once again. A mile or so down the road, the ol' mare done the same thing again. Again, too, the ol' boy stopped the wagon and walked around to the horse. "That's twice," he said. Well, they got a-goin' once again, but hadn't gone more'n a couple more miles when darned if that mare didn't go and do the same thing. This time when the ol' boy walked up to the horse, he didn't say nary a word. He just whipped out his ol' pistol and shot her clean through the head. Needless to say, his new bride was shocked. As he climbed back into the wagon she started in on him with, "How could you go and do a thing like that? The mare didn't do it a-purpose. Now how're we supposed to get home?" The ol' boy didn't miss a beat, but turned to his new wife, looked her right in the eye, and said "That's once."

This ol' boy who'd spent most of his life livin' like he was the bigger part of half outlaw took a notion to straighten up his life and get saved. With this noble aim in mind, he took hisself to a tent revival meetin'. He walked right up the middle aisle to the preacher in front of God and the whole congregation and said, "Preacher, I'm a bone-deep sinner. I been drinkin' for nigh on to thirty years and when I get sauced up I been knowed to beat around some on my lovin' wife." "Hallelujah," said the preacher. "Tell it all, brother, tell it all." "Well," continued the encouraged sinner, "there's been times when I was out and saw a pretty young thing and just couldn't resist the urge to gather her up and spend the night with her." "Tell it all, brother, tell it all," shouted the preacher. Diggin' deep into his soul, the sinner pulled out his final confession. "Preacher, once I even got so low that I went to bed with a man." "Ooh," said the preacher, "I don't believe I'd a told that."

There was once this ol' boy a-sittin' mindin' his own business at the local joint when his best friend come rollin' in and made straight for his table. The best friend, not feelin' no pain, said, "I heard tell that you been a-spreadin' the rumor around town that you been sleepin' with my wife and that you been a-provin' it by tellin' folks about the mole she's got right below her belly button." The first ol' boy got real upset real quick and said, "Now, I'm a-tellin you. That's exactly how them ol' nasty rumors get started. I never said she *had* a mole there. I said it *looked like* a mole."

Pa Jones decided that after forty years of bein' married up with Ma Jones, he'd just about enjoyed all he could stand of her. He took hisself to town and asked his ol' buddy Doc Rayburn how he might go about killin' her off without hurtin' her none. Doc suggested that Pa drink up a love potion he had on hand, go on to the house, and just plumb wear Ma out of the picture a-makin' love to her. Doc guaranteed that Ma wouldn't be able to last out a minute over sixty days. About forty-five days later, Doc rode out to the Jones' place to see how the plan was progressin'. He found Ma out in the garden a-hoein' her tomatoes, just a-singin' and a-grinnin' and really a-gittin' after it. Pa, on the other hand, was a-sittin' on the porch so weak and drawed out that he couldn't hardly even spit, no less rock. Doc got kinely worried and asked Pa how

things was a-goin' with him. "I'm fine," answered Pa in a faint voice, "but look at that ol' fool out there, won't you? She ain't got the faintest idea in the world that she's got only fifteen days left on this earth."

This ol' politician runnin' for county commissioner was testifyin' pretty stout to a local crowd of folks at a campaign bar-b-que. All of a sudden, one of the wives in the crowd jumped up and hollered out, "How can you expect us to vote for you when everybody in town knows you been sleepin' with Sallie Mae Dingus, and the two of you married, but not to each other?" "That's a flat out lie," the politican shot back. "We never slept a wink."

Ol' Jim Bob run over to his neighbor's place to ask if he might borry his mule for the day, seein' as his own'd took sick the evenin' before. "Sure enough," said the neighbor, "but I don't want you mistreatin' him none." Jim Bob agreed to treat him right, and the neighbor went on out into the pasture, gathered him up, and slipped a harness on him. Then he reached down and picked up an ol' two-by-four a-layin' at his feet and caught the mule one hell of a wallop with it right between the eyes. "Hold on there," said Jim Bob. "I thought you said he wasn't to be mistreated." "You darn sure got that right," answered the neighbor, "but first you kinely got to get his attention."

This ol' spinster woman moved to the country from out of New York City and set her up a poultry farm. When the county agent dropped in to say howdy, he saw right off that she was a mite confused: she'd bought a hundred hens and a hundred roosters. "Ma'am," he began, "I'm not a-tryin' to tell you your business, but you only need two or three roosters to cover them hens." "I realize that," she snapped right back, "but I don't want one of those hens to suffer as I have."

This ol' widder woman whose husband had been gone for a good many years was takin' a trip to visit her young 'uns when Jesse James and his outlaw band stopped the train.

Jesse himself announced to the passengers that he was a-goin' to rob all the men and make free with all the women. A dignified ol' gentleman from town jumped up and said, "Sir, you may indeed rob all the men, but you are not going to take advantage of these good and helpless women." The ol' widder woman turned to the gentleman and said, "Who's a-robbin' this train, anyways? You let Jesse tend to his own business."

REDNECK MASCOT: THE ARMADILLO

It's a funny thing about armadillos. They got to be the only animal you see more often layin' dead by the side of the road than walkin' around livin'. Seems there's three dead 'dillos to every dead possum or skunk you pass goin' just about anywhere. They got a real bad habit of tryin' like blazes to cross the road to get to the other side and not quite makin' it most of the time. They ain't fast, but they sure got stickin' power; they keep on a-tryin' even though the odds are dead against 'em.

Although folks with gardens, flower beds, cows and horses in pasture, and manicured yards get kinely hostile when you mention the 'dillo on account of his real fondness for diggin' big ol' holes whenever and wherever he takes a notion to, we feel they're the perfect mascot for rednecks everywhere. Like us, it seems modern times (in the particular form of cars and pickups), is aimin' to eliminate 'em, but they keep a-goin' on. Like us, too, they got a hard, armorlike coverin' on the outside and are just as soft and sweet as you please on the inside.

Texans seem to think they got exclusive rights to the armadillo, but that ain't quite so. The 'dillo did *not*, just like a lot of things you prob'ly heard tell *did*, originate in Texas. Actually, they wasn't born real Americans at all. They wandered up from South America and liked it so much they've settled in for the duration. Obviously, what they're a-lackin' in longevity they make up for in good sense. They're pretty much scattered all over the south and southwest now.

It don't hardly seem right to go too hard on the 'dillo for the diggin' he does. Since they ain't mean enough to fight back and ain't real swift of foot, they developed this talent to escape from animals more interested in havin' 'em for dinner than in gettin' acquainted.

Anyways, the 'dillo is puttin' in his appearance in many more places than the side of the road these days. Frankly, he looks a whole lot better on a belt buckle than on the pavement. Seems like folks can't help bein' charmed by them. Leastways, they must like how they look 'cause them little artichokes of the animal kingdom is decoratin' everything from hat tacks to shoes, and likenesses of 'em now can be got in anything from brass to wood. We've gathered up a collection of what the Frenchies might call *objets d'artadillos* so's you can see what we mean.

10

Looky Here: Pichur Models You Can Pattern Yourself After

THE HONKY TONK ANGEL

◀THE QUEEN OF THE DEW DROP INN

MAMA

THE WIFE

THE SWEET YOUNG THING

THE GOOD OL' GIRL

THE COWBOY

THE ROUGHNECK

THE DRUG STORE COWBOY

THE GOOD OL' BOY

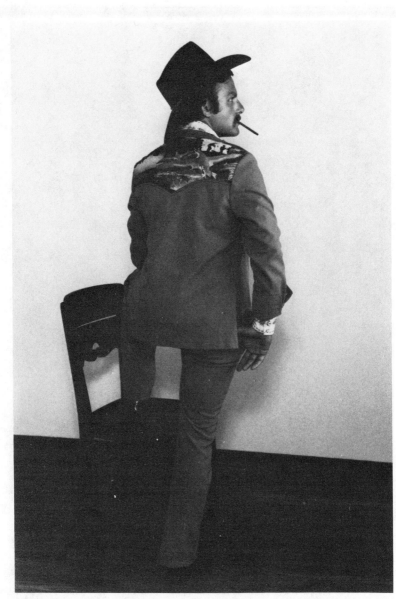

THE URBAN COWBOY

THE WORKIN' MAN